573
WAYS TO
SAVE
MONEY

573
WAYS TO
SAVE
MONEY

Save the Cost of This Book Many
Times Over in Less than a Day!

Peter Sander and Jennifer Sander

THE LYONS PRESS
Guilford, Connecticut
An imprint of the Globe Pequot Press

Text designed by Sheryl P. Kober

Library of Congress Cataloging-in-Publication Data is available on file.

ISBN 978-1-59921-850-2

Printed in the United States of America

10 9 8 7 6 5 4 3 2 1

Get used to it—the party is over.

After years of what seemed like a nonstop economic boom, growth in our standard of living, and endless opportunities to move up, um, well, that is no longer the case.

Your main responsibility now—to yourself, your family, and your future—is to make what money you still have in your life go farther and last longer. Sometimes that will mean not spending it at all. Sometimes that will mean finding ways to get what you want for less. And sometimes it will mean swallowing your pride and asking a friend or neighbor for a bit of help. When even the President's wife wears clothes from the Gap and J. Crew and decorates with furniture from Pottery Barn, there is no reason to hide your thrifty ways or be embarrassed about trying to make your money go farther. We are all in the same boat. Let's get right to work then, and start saving money.

—Peter and Jennifer Sander

"It is easy to meet expenses—everywhere we go, there they are."

—Anonymous

Use regular gas.

Sure, any fancy car will tell you in the owner's manual that you must, must use premium gas in your car or terrible things will happen. "When I first bought my Range Rover," our friend Bob Slobe told us, "I only used premium gas, just like the manual said. Then I sat next to a judge at a dinner party who was explaining a case in which a gas company had been forced to admit that the type of gas really didn't affect the engine's performance. I started using regular that next day." The difference in price between premium and regular is usually around 20 cents, which adds up when you are filling an eighteen-gallon tank. And when you are filling your tank week in and week out, the cost difference is considerable. So go ahead and take the regular gas plunge. Keep the money in your wallet instead of in your tank. And speaking of keeping the money, fifteen years later, Bob is still driving the same car.

Pump up your tires.

Remember the days when you rode a bicycle (and we hope you still do), and those tires weren't quite pumped up enough? It seemed like you were slogging through mud— hard crank after hard crank, and the bike slowed to a crawl between cranks. Well, your car rides much the same way. Poorly inflated tires make your engine work harder. And guess what? You use more gas—perhaps as much as 10 percent more. EPA studies suggest that properly inflated tires save 1 to 2 miles per gallon. Taken over time that's a lot. So keep a pressure gauge handy, and if you're lucky, you'll find a service station with free air nearby.

Hang your clothes out to dry.

Your clothes dryer uses a lot of energy, roughly 5 to 10 percent of total residential energy use. By making one simple change, you can reduce the amount of power you pay for each month. Even if you only hang your clothes outside during the summer, it can make a real difference in your yearly bill.

Your family might complain that air-dried things are stiff (and they will be right). To get around that, Jennifer tosses air-dried laundry into the dryer for just a few minutes. Okay, so she is using the dryer, but it is for five minutes instead of fifty. Big difference in how much that will cost.

Although Jennifer's drying rack came from the local hardware store, you can find a good source for clotheslines at www.clotheslineshop.com or www.urbanclothesline.com (type "clotheslines" in the search window).

Change the air filter in your car.

Imagine running a marathon wearing one of those little dust masks people use for sanding wood or other home projects. Now imagine it's clogged with dirt. You'd suffer. You'd wheeze and gasp for precious air. It's the same with your car. A dirty air filter can reduce your fuel economy by up to 10 percent. A clean one not only will boost your car's fuel efficiency, but make it run better too. For most cars, it's an easy fix—two to four clips, maybe a screw or wing nut or two, and an $8 or $10 filter from your neighborhood auto parts store. You can do it yourself in less than five minutes on most cars. When in doubt, ask the guy or gal behind the counter at the parts store.

Hand wash instead of dry clean.

Dry cleaning bills are big—we all know that. Some professional clothes like suits and ties can't be cleaned any other way. But for other items we have options, and one of them is to get our hands wet at home.

Sweaters, lingerie, knitted dresses. Take a careful look in your closet to see what kinds of things you can clean yourself. You will read later that we are big fans of using cloth napkins, but not the kind you have to have cleaned. Chances are you can hand wash and press your own linen napkins.

For the items you can't clean at home, try to stretch their use before your visit to the dry cleaners. Unless you've dripped something onto your pants or smeared something on a sweater, an extra wearing or two won't be obvious to anyone but you. Maybe it is time to put the dry-clean-only clothes at the back of the closet and use something else for daily use.

"Annual income twenty pounds, annual expenditure nineteen pounds nineteen and six, result happiness. Annual income twenty pounds, annual expenditure twenty pounds ought and six, result misery."

—Charles Dickens, David Copperfield

Learn to use a solar cooker.

Jennifer saw her first solar cooker years ago at an artist's garden party. He'd cooked the main-course chicken with a solar oven he'd built himself. "Hmmmm," she thought, "That could be kind of fun." She never did build her own (someday . . .) but did buy an inexpensive solar cooker through www.solarcookers.org and uses it frequently during the summer months. Basically, it is a solar slow cooker, and any kind of dish that you can make in an electric slow cooker can be made in a solar cooker too.

Why? Well, why not keep the electricity off as much as you can in the months when it costs the most to use? By using a solar cooker to make dinner for her family (baked chicken, pot roast, slow-cooked pork), she can keep the family energy use under the point at which higher rates get triggered. In the summer of 2008, by air drying the clothes and using a solar cooker for many meals, she cut our power bill to half of what it had been the summer before. Another money bonus is that slow cooking methods allow you to use less-expensive cuts of meat: Hours and hours in the pot make them as tender as more expensive choices.

Go meatless twice a week.

Ours is not a vegetarian household. Peter is from the Midwest, and Jennifer loves a juicy slice of prime rib. But for cost reasons, and for health, we try to have a few meatless meals every week. Alas, we don't mean fish instead of meat, as fish is usually even more expensive. No, it is rice and beans that do the trick. Casseroles, burritos, quesadillas, veggie stir-fries—you name it, and we can make it.

You can find amazing ideas on www.meatlessmonday.com, a site filled with recipes and health information about the benefits of cutting back your meat consumption. Bypass the fish recipes if going meatless is a money thing for you, and focus instead on the casseroles, bakes, and the pasta bowls, and do check out the "Meatless Jambalaya" recipe.

Bake your own bread.

If you are addicted to the beautiful artisan loaves in specialty bakeries, you will be delighted to know that you can make them yourself. Really, you can. And a loaf will cost you less than a dollar, rather than the four or five you'd pay for a fresh loaf in a bakery. The secret is to use the recipe in an amazing book called *Artisan Bread in Five Minutes a Day*. Jennifer read the recipe in the food section of the *New York Times* over a year ago and has literally made hundreds of loaves ever since (despite her lack of baking talent).

The most expensive ingredient is yeast. Flour, water, and kosher salt are the only other ingredients. The master recipe can also be used for pizza dough, sweet breads like cinnamon rolls, and sandwich rolls. You can find the simple recipe and instructions online. Visit www.motherearthnews.com and search for "artisan bread in five minutes a day." Jennifer is such a fan of this book, however, that she believes you should run out and buy a copy. Or at least look for it in your local library.

Five minutes a day. That is all you need to save money and have your own inexpensive, flavorful, homemade bread. And your house will smell wonderful.

"I've noticed that people who don't respect money don't have any."

—J. Paul Getty

Make two meals out of one.

You know how to do this; everyone does. It is just that you might have gotten out of the habit of doing it in the past few years. Time to look anew at what you can do with the leftovers.

Roast a chicken one night, then use the carcass to make soup stock and the bits of left-over chicken to make burritos (fill it up with beans, rice, corn, and lima beans). Bake a pork roast one night, and use the leftovers for barbeque sandwiches the next (with buns you've made yourself, of course, from the master bread recipe you just learned about!). If you spent $10 on the original piece of meat and make it last for a second meal, you will look like an economic genius who can feed a family for mere pennies.

Out of ideas? Ask your mom. Call your grandmother. Walk next door and ask a neighbor for a recipe. Your children will also have great recipe suggestions for leftovers, but they might all involve ice cream.

Form a swap pool with your neighbors.

Look around you at the things you own—boats, trailers, RVs, swimming pools, lawn mowers, woodworking tools. Now think about what your neighbors own—that second house at the lake, a photo printer, a Wii and the games to go with it, exercise equipment. If there is something you need that they have, doesn't it make sense to try to arrange a temporary swap or exchange rather than going out to buy or rent it? And if they in turn needed something you owned, wouldn't you be happy to swap the use of your trailer for a weekend at their lake house?

Invite them all over one evening to talk about this idea. Sharing and swapping with our neighbors might seem radical at first, but it has ancient roots and is far more common during times of economic stress. Chances are your neighbors have been thinking about it too and will be delighted and relieved that you are the one who has stepped up to organize.

"Money is a terrible master but an excellent servant."

—P. T. Barnum

Rent things you don't need year-round.

Okay, so maybe your neighbors don't have everything you need, and sometimes you won't be able to arrange a swap. That doesn't mean you should march out and make a big purchase for something that you won't actually use that much. Yes, we all like to own; of course we do. But it makes more sense moneywise to rent big items only for the time we need them (the trailer to move grandma home, the chipper shredder to clean up after a storm). The big purchases that many made in the past few years—the RVs, the boats, the vacation homes—really don't pencil out well even in the best of times. Better to hang on to your cash, keep your credit line manageable, and be clear-eyed about how much use those things will really get over the course of a year.

Shop your girlfriend's closet.

Tired of what you own, but trying to stay out of the mall? It's a quandary. Chances are your friends are feeling it too, and you can help each other out. Suggest an afternoon get-together in which everyone brings over several items that they aren't wearing any longer. Spread them all out, and "shop" each other's unused clothing. That old red sweater you haven't worn in years might be just the thing a friend needs to perk up her tired blue jeans. And her black blazer would go so well with your tweed pants.... End the afternoon feeling proud that no one spent money and that you found new homes for clothes you no longer need.

Buy half bottles of wine.

True confession time: We find it hard to stay out of the wine aisle, even in these nutty times. California reds make our hearts sing, but the prices can stop the music cold. What to do? Start drinking the cheap stuff? Sure, we do stock up on plenty of the $3 and $4 bottles at the grocery stores, but we also keep an eye out for good wines in small bottles—at www.halfwitwines.com.

The huge selection of half bottles at this site will let you drink the big labels you love, but in smaller quantities for a lower price. Among our favorite brands available in half bottles are Cakebread, Del Dotto, Duckhorn, and Stag's Leap. So instead of spending $60 on a bottle of Stag's Leap, buy a half bottle for a special occasion, spend $26, and satisfy that good wine urge.

"Money is like water: Too little creates a desert, too much a flood. Only in the right proportion does it give life."

—Judith Green

Organize potluck dinner parties.

No need to feel like you have to eliminate all social activity until the economy perks back up. In fact, what better time to gather your friends around and revel in the glow of friendship? Putting out a spread for cocktails and appetizers does add up though, so instead, why not organize a potluck dinner party and have a party for the same amount it takes to feed a family for one night? Real comfort food is called for at times like this.

Coordinate with each other to make sure you have all of your party bases covered—snacks, salads, beverages, main dish, sides—and don't forget dessert. You don't want to end up with three taco casseroles and nothing else. Let your guests know that this is about getting together for a good time, not a competition to see who can bring the fanciest dish. Spend your money on simple things, and focus on each other.

"Contrary to F. Scott Fitzgerald's claim, the rich really aren't all that different from you and me—with one major exception: They're an awful lot more careful about how they spend and invest their money."

—Thomas J. Stanley and William D. Danko

Barter or trade for what you need.

Do you have a skill or specialized knowledge? If so, you might be able to trade or barter to get what you need. Jennifer trades her homemade bread (such a useful skill!) for yoga lessons from one neighbor and fresh vegetables from another. She has also traded her advertising copywriting skills to local restaurants in exchange for meals, and once accepted wine instead of a consulting fee. If you're approaching a business, be sure you are talking to the owner, or a person who can cut a deal. Think hard about what you could offer—perhaps a locally owned store needs your help with signage or a window display in exchange for the product you want, or you could offer accounting help in exchange for store credit. What about offering to help a business owner at home—with cooking or cleaning—in exchange for needed items? Even if all you can offer is your time and strong back, give it a try. Perhaps the manager needs an extra hand moving stock one day. Craigslist has a barter section; look under "For Sale." Among this Web site's recent offered trades were residential landscaping in exchange for help with a business Web site design, and for firewood, offers from several folks for items like a treadmill and a scooter.

Always, always, ask for a discount.

Get over your shyness. No matter where you are, no matter what you are trying to buy, always ask for a discount. No one will be shocked or offended; in fact, they are probably expecting it. Even large stores are open to shaving something off the price if you ask the right way. "Is this scheduled to go on sale anytime soon?" you ask, and if it is, wonder aloud if you can have that price now. Asking "Is that your best price?" or "Can you do any better on the price?" also helps to get the conversation going.

If you feel comfortable inserting your own needs into the conversation, you can also try the old "Hmm, that is more than I was planning to spend . . ." and see if they take up the conversation from there with a lower price. And if they won't move on the price, go ahead and check out their competitors to see if they will come down a bit.

"An economist is an expert who will know tomorrow why the things he predicted yesterday didn't happen."

—Earl Wilson

Go wild with your salads.

Now here is an old piece of country wisdom: Some of what grows wild in your yard is edible. It won't feed a family, but it will stretch a salad. You can pick dandelion greens, wild lettuce, pansies, and mustard greens, among others. Don't pick from a yard that uses pesticides, and stay away from wild mushrooms unless you are knowledgeable, as they can be deadly.

In the late winter and early spring, Jennifer adds miner's lettuce and tiny purple pansies to her salad. She also cooks up a batch or two of dandelion greens flavored with garlic and onions. Wild-food fans will tell you these wild plants have great nutritional value, higher sometimes than commercially grown produce. And you'll feel like a real pioneer, scanning the horizon for something edible and free.

Save money on gift cards.

Here is a good way to save 15 to 20 percent when buying gift cards from major stores: Buy them online at www.gift cardsagain.com. Buying them in-store requires you to pay face value, but using this site will make your money go farther. If you plan to give gift cards as gifts, check out what you can find here: Bloomingdale's, Borders Books, major movie-theater chains, and more.

What to do with those gift cards you received but don't really want or need? Cash them in, of course, on a site that is run by the same company: www.giftcardbuyback.com will tell you the three steps you need to follow to convert your cards to a check in the mail.

Bring your lunch to work and school.

Like cooking with leftovers, we all know how to do this but have gotten out of the habit. Time to begin again, starting now. A lunch out every day can add up to $100 a week or more, depending on your tastes. Bringing your own lunch in a bag every day? Closer to $20 a week, depending on what you decide to eat. And don't forget gas; even if you drive out for cheap fast food, you are burning up gas you won't use walking down the hall to the refrigerator. Save money, save gas, and there is a good chance you will also lose weight eating your own homemade lunch rather than one bought in a store or restaurant.

Invest in a nice, hard-sided lunch pail so you don't end up with smashed sandwiches and bruised fruit. Sandwiches will only cost about $2 to make, and if you think creatively, you can come up with great low-cost menus that will prevent you from feeling deprived. Cold pasta or rice salads are inexpensive and can be made in big batches; leftover soups and stews can be brought in a sturdy, leak-proof Thermos; and wraps with tortillas or lettuce leaves will cost far less than their restaurant counterparts.

"Today, there are three kinds of people: the have's, the have-not's, and the have-not-paid-for-what-they-have's."

—Earl Wilson

Use rechargeable batteries.

Americans use and dispose of some 15 billion batteries per year. Now aside from being an environmental problem, these little guys can run you up some pretty big bills, particularly if you buy them from expensive convenience or grocery stores. If you have a device, say a music player, a PDA, or digital camera that uses "AA" cells or some other common format, rechargeable "NiMH" (nickel-metal hydride, for you techies) can save a bunch. A charger might run $40 and a pair of batteries $4 or so, but over time, the savings will add up.

Buy big-ticket items out of season.

Need a pair of skis or a snowboard? Best to buy them in April. A boat? Try mid-winter. Looking for a deal on a car? Show up at the dealership in November. Sweaters and coats? Try when the weather turns springlike. The tail end of a season is the best time to look as retailers want to move merchandise to make room for the next hot new thing. Selection will be limited to what they have left, but the savings will make up for it.

This is a good reason to plan ahead, because if you can anticipate your need for something big and buy it ahead of when you need it, chances are you will get a much better price. Feel free to ask salespeople in the store about the best time to buy. Everyone likes to be seen as an expert and show off insider knowledge, even if it costs them a sale.

Holiday savings abound.

Sherry Crum, who manages a Northern California La-Z-Boy recliner store, says that "Any of the holiday sales (Thanksgiving, President's Day, Labor Day, Easter, Christmas, etc.) generally offers opportunities for better deals. Furniture can be sold for less during those periods as it is made up in sales volume. Also, keep an eye out for special ads and flyers; some stores will offer great promotions."

Haunt garage sales.

Maybe what you need isn't in a store, but in someone else's driveway with a big "For Sale" sticker on it. Garage sales can yield all kinds of low-cost goodies; you just never know what you will find. As this book is about hanging on to your cash, we don't mean to encourage you to spend a Saturday morning in mindless garage-sale mode, picking up wacky stuff that no one else wants and you really don't need, but dang, it is too cheap to pass up!

Decide in advance what it is you are seeking, and stick to your plan. If you need bookshelves, only look at bookshelves, not at used toasters. Get a conversation going with the folks holding the garage sale. If you tell them you are in the market for something they hadn't thought of selling, perhaps they will decide to offer it up. Buyer beware, of course, when buying off the pavement in front of someone's house. The TV you just bought might stop working tomorrow, and then what would you do? No warranty, no guarantee. Think carefully and ask questions before you buy something that can break.

Hold your own garage sale.

Maybe it is time for you to generate a little cash too, and hold a garage sale of your own. How exactly will this save you money? If you de-clutter and clear things out of your life that you no longer need, you might breathe a little easier and not be so stressed about the future. If you sell things that need regular fixing or upkeep, you will save yourself those fees. Ridding yourself of excess junk might also eliminate the need to pay costly monthly storage fees to store the stuff you don't need or use.

Find spa bargains at beauty schools.

Jennifer is a fan of pedicures and facials. She is also a fan of not paying the high price at a fancy spa. So she seeks out beauty schools where students offer what fancy spas do, but for far less. To find a school near you, type "cosmetology school" and your nearest big city into a search engine. You can also ask your own beauty operator where he or she went to school and about possible bargains to be had. Instead of losing a customer to a student they just might cut their own price.

Find bargain massages too.

Just like you can get a less expensive pedicure through a beauty school, you can save money on massages by finding a massage school in your area. To find a school near you, type "massage school" and your nearest big city into a search engine. How much can you save? At the International Professional School of Bodywork in San Diego, you can get a sixty-minute massage from a skilled student for only $45—less than a dollar a minute for bliss. Sounds good to us.

Buy three to get one free.

If you can't find a beauty school or massage school in your area, you might try approaching your local spa and asking about a price break if you buy a number of services. "If I buy three massages, will you throw in a fourth one for free?" or "If I buy three pedicures, can I have the fourth one free?" Many businesses, not just those in the beauty and spa trade, will be happy to go for this. They get a bigger chunk of money up front and keep happy customers, who will recommend them to friends.

"Do not be fooled into believing that because a man is rich he is necessarily smart. There is ample proof to the contrary."

—Julius Rosenwald

Check out the back of the paint s'

A gallon of paint isn't cheap, but there is a way ᴛᴏ .
bargains in the paint department. For small jobs, when you
only need a can or two, ask if they have any "mistints." These
are cans of paint from a large order that didn't turn out
quite right— a slightly off beige, or a blue that had an extra
drop of yellow in it. You might be able to find colors that will
do the trick for your bathroom or hallway at less than half
the price of custom paint. Call your local hardware store or
paint stores to see who has mistints they'd like to get rid of.

Ask yourself—can I find this used?

When you realize that you in are need of something, no
matter what, stop and ask yourself—can I find this used?
The price difference between a new car and a slightly used
one will pay for your gas for the year. The price difference
between a new snowboard and a used snowboard will pay
for more than one lift ticket. The price difference between
a new bicycle and a used bicycle will easily pay for a new
helmet (you don't want to buy a used one of those!), some
extra inner tubes, and a strong lock. The price difference
between a used DVD and a new DVD will pay for the bottle
of wine you drink while watching it.

Here is the secret: It really doesn't matter that it is used.
Get over your idea that it is somehow tainted. If you buy
something used, no one needs to know except you. Go
ahead and keep that info to yourself and let your friends
wonder how you can still afford to buy a car, a snowboard, a
bicycle, and a bunch of DVDs.

Learn to freecycle.

Want to get something for nothing? Then join your local "freecycle" group. Yes, there are lots of folks out there who just want someone to come and take something they no longer need—like the woman in my local freecycle group with an 8-by-10-foot tent that she didn't have room for, "so the first person to want it can take it." Pretty cool for someone in need of a tent, wouldn't you say? To see what is being offered free to a good home in your area, go to www .freecyle.org and search for a group near you. Once you join (free membership, of course) you will also be able to list the things that are cluttering up your life that you would be happy to have someone come and take for free.

Wake up your garden with Starbucks.

Coffee grounds are good for your garden. Who has coffee grounds that they need to get rid of? Why, Starbucks, of course. Many Starbucks locations bag up the used coffee grounds and offer them for free to any interested gardener who asks. So ask, and start feeding your soil for free.

Free tomato seeds.

The Campbell Soup company is encouraging everyone to plant a vegetable garden by giving out free packets of seeds. The seeds are for the special Roma tomato that they use in their classic Tomato Soup. To get your free seeds, you will need to buy one can of any Campbell's condensed soup and follow the directions at www.helpgrowyoursoup.com.

Stay home for board games with friends and family.

The cost of going out for dinner and a movie can add up, if you have a family, and you may end up spending well over $100 by the time you get back home. To cut costs, plan a family game night instead.

You already have the games; of course you do. They are up on the high shelf in the closet—the boxes of Monopoly and Scrabble, and who knows what else. And if you don't have them, you can pick them up for just a few dollars at a garage sale, always a reliable source for old board games.

Plan special snacks, choose your family's favorite music, spread them out on the table or floor, and enjoy!

Look for antique bargains.

Check out the biggest antique and flea market in the country. Items stretching out over a mile are sold at Brimfield, Massachusetts (www.brimfield.com). It happens only three times a year for several days at a time in May, July, and September.

Is there a similar but smaller market near you on the weekends? If so, you will find a big source of bargain furniture, collectibles, and other oddities. Don't like the sticker price on something you want? Get ready to bargain and see if you can end up with a better price. Bring cash with you, as offering to pay by cash always gets you the best price.

Learn to love consignment stores.

Jennifer has a closet full of top designer labels like Chanel and Escada. Rest assured she paid nowhere near the thousands it would cost to buy these outfits new. No, she haunts designer consignment stores around the country on a continuous search for designer bargains. The best stores are in wealthy towns or neighborhoods. New York's Upper East Side has many, including Second Chance and Michael's; Los Angeles boasts Decades. But also look in smaller upscale centers like Carmel, California, or the wine country town of St. Helena, California, where you might find Jennifer looking through the racks.

To find a designer consignment store near you, type "designer consignment" and the nearest big city into your search engine. You never know what you will find . . .

Ask about free admission.

Museums are a wonderful way to spend an afternoon soaking in some visual beauty or learning about cultural history. Many museums have a sliding scale for admission, and if you ask, you might learn about "free days" when the admission is waived altogether. In Denver, for instance, the Denver Museum of Nature & Science has a free day once a month. Look on your local museum's Web site for information on upcoming free days.

The Metropolitan Museum of Art in New York "suggests" an admission price of $20, but it is perfectly okay for you to pay less if you can't afford it. *Smithsonian Magazine* organizes a large, nationwide, Free Museum Day. You can find the information for the 2009 date (it hasn't yet been announced) on their Web site at http://microsite.smithsonianmag.com/museumday/.

Make friends with your library.

"Gee, isn't there a library around here somewhere?" Chances are there is one near you, and this is the time for you to reacquaint yourself with its offerings. Books, of course, are what first come to mind, and there are thousands that you haven't yet read that can be checked out for free. But there are also magazines to read, computers to use, and DVDs, CDs, and audio books to borrow as well.

Children's read-aloud programs are great for a rainy day, and many libraries also have a community room that you can book to use for a meeting. Go on, head to the library and see what is going on there since the last time you went. We guarantee you will be back once you realize the tremendous savings potential of your local library.

Indulge in homemade chocolate truffles.

Chocolate truffles are deliciously, and sadly, expensive. Just a few can easily cost $10. But for closer to $8, you can make your own. Imagine, an entire batch of truffles to share with friends, or not, according to your mood. The most expensive ingredients you will need are heavy cream and baking chocolate.

You can spend an afternoon of creative fun in your own kitchen making up a batch of chocolate truffles. Simple to make, truffles can be created using a variety of recipes. Find them online by typing "chocolate truffle recipe" into your search engine.

Ramp up the caloric indulgence level by rolling your truffles in crushed candies or chopped nuts, or make a grown-up-only version by adding flavored liqueurs. Either way you will have far more chocolate for your money than you could get buying that gold-foil embossed box full of fancy truffles.

"Learn from the mistakes of others. You won't live long enough to make them all yourself."

—Jane Bryant Quinn

"A deficit is what you have when you haven't got as much as you had when you had nothing."

—Gerald F. Lieberman

Save money on mattresses.

Before you put out the money for a brand new mattress—and those can easily run in the thousands—ask the sales person if they have any "mismatched sets." JT Long used to own a chain of mattress stores and told us, "Just like cars, the manufacturers come out with new styles each year. This leads to big savings when the retailers have to get rid of the old inventory so the mattresses delivered will match the one on the showroom floor."

Hey, that doesn't matter, because the ugly, clearance fabric will be covered with sheets. When purchasing a mismatched set, be sure that the box spring really has springs and is not a solid foundation—a plywood platform covered in fabric. That will cause your mattress to wear out faster because it doesn't provide any give.

Soak at home for less.

Our same source on mattress bargains, JT Long, is now in the spa business and shared this on how to get a bargain price on a big-ticket item. "Again, like cars, spa manufacturers come out with new models every year. In the winter, November through February, dealers are hungry because business is slower and they have old inventory to get out of the warehouse. If you are not picky about color, and will take a spa in stock, you can save thousands. Winter home shows and summer fairs are another time when retailers have purchased inventory at discounted prices and will pass that savings on to customers."

Today's home spas save money by being more energy efficient and requiring fewer chemicals to stay clean, thanks to enhanced insulation and innovations such as ozonators. Features worth paying more for include a pressure-treated base that will withstand the elements. A $10,000 spa on a rotted base will not enhance relaxation. Carefully balance your desire for magic bubble fingers with price. The more jets, the more motor is required, and the more expensive the spa will be to purchase and to run. Other additions such as sound systems and flat-screen television monitors can make the purchase costly and increase the chances of repairs later on.

Fill up on soup and split your meals.

Restaurant meals can really add up, and budget-minded folks are best to avoid them if at all possible. But hey, every once in a while you just need to get out. To really save on a restaurant tab for two, try ordering a cup of soup for each of you as an appetizer, and then splitting a main course. Restaurant food is served in huge portions, and in many places a meal for one can easily become a meal for two. Peter and Jennifer frequently enjoy a special night out by splitting a big prime rib dinner.

Shop the outside aisles of the grocery store.

Marcie Rothman of San Diego is known as the Five Dollar Chef, specializing in helping families stretch their budgets. Her single biggest piece of advice for anyone about to walk through the doors of a grocery store is to stick to the outside aisles. The outside perimeter of a grocery store is where you will find fresh items like meats, dairy, and vegetables. If you limit your spending to meat, produce, and dairy, and skip strolling up and down the aisles filled with expensive prepackaged products, you will spend less. "Making your own food is healthier, and it doesn't take any longer to cook real food than to prepare something out of a box."

Put on a wine-tasting party.

Wine can be expensive. So instead of giving up on those nights when you have one or two special bottles of wine, why not invite your friends to join you in a BYOB wine-tasting party. You each buy one nice bottle, and everyone enjoys the variety without the big bill at the end of an evening. Jennifer had a successful champagne-tasting party during the holidays, and it only cost her $40 for her one bottle of champagne.

"Home wine-tasting parties can be very fun and creative," Roxanne Langer of WineFUNdamentals says. "Once you choose a theme, you can ask your guests to bring a bottle based on the theme."

Roll your own (candles, that is).

Beeswax candles are beautiful but aren't cheap. You can buy the material you need to "roll your own" at any local beekeeping supply store and make a pair of hand-rolled candles for $1 a piece. Compared to the $4 a pair you'd pay in a gift store, that's a real bargain. If you can't find the supplies near you, Sacramento Beekeeping, www.sacramentobeekeeping .com, ships all over the country.

Not only are these fun to make and use in your own home, but hand-rolled candles also make great gifts. "You made these yourself? Really?" Yes, you really did, for half of the retail price!

Tomatoes—try your beginning gardener's luck.

Getting started growing a vegetable garden can be intimidating. But give tomatoes a try—they really aren't that hard. You can grow them from seed if you really want the full experience or buy small starter plants early in the spring. One tomato plant will run around $4, and when fully grown and producing, will keep you in tomatoes all summer long. With the cost of produce, particularly organic produce, it is a bargain investment. Eat your tomatoes fresh, roasted on sandwiches, or make your own spaghetti sauce. If your garden produces enough, you can try canning and enjoy your summer tomatoes all winter long next year. Choose the sunniest part of your garden and see what you can do. Check out www.helpfulgardener.com for advice on growing tomatoes.

Ask your friends for garden cuttings.

Envious of a friend's beautiful garden but without the cash to invest in lots of new plants? Why not ask your friend if you can have cuttings from their garden and grow your own from theirs? Jennifer has had great success with cuttings from rosemary plants, and has started a small vineyard with cuttings from a friend's already producing Cabernet vines. For free. Herbs and wine for free, does it get any better than that?

Good candidates for cuttings are: hydrangeas, herbs like basil, sage, and mint, fruit trees, and berries. Check out www.helpfulgardener.com for more info on getting started with cuttings and plant a garden for free.

Make your own cat toys.

Holly Tse was looking for ways to amuse her cats without spending money. Her efforts led her to write a book, *Make Your Own Cat Toys,* and put up a Web site, www.make yourowncattoys.com, which is filled with useful ideas.

You will never again spend money on expensive cat toys from a store once you try a few of her clever ideas. Holly focused on using things already lying around the house. For instance, our cats' favorite, Ring Toss, is made from a cardboard toilet paper roll. Just cut one up into small cardboard rings and start tossing them to your cat.

Learn simple upholstery techniques.

Furniture looking a tad shabby? If it will cost too much to replace it right now, why not try to perk it up with a little reupholstery? Fabric scraps can be had in the remnant sections of fabric stores and craft stores like Jo-Ann for just a few dollars, and it is not hard to freshen up footstools and chair bottoms using just scissors, fabric, upholstery nails, or a staple gun. Jennifer recently spent $5 to redo two dining room chair seat cushions with velvet fabric and a staple gun. Simple step-by-step information can be found on www .motherearthnews.com. You can also check to see if the local adult learning center near you teaches an upholstery class. It is a skill worth learning—one that could save you hundreds of dollars throughout the years.

Mow your own lawn.

If you're a homeowner you may be like many who decided that mowing the lawn was boring, hot work and there were better things to do with free time anyway. You decided to turn it over to a neighborhood kid (if you were lucky enough to find one) for $20, or if you're like most of us and couldn't find one, you hired more professional labor at about $40, $50, or more a week. That's a lot of money for an hour's worth of work. Consider "de-outsourcing" it—you'll save, you'll get some useful exercise, and a strengthened "pride-of-ownership" feeling too.

Have "no-drive" days.

We've all become so dependent on our cars that it seems we go somewhere almost every day. If we're a couple, we both go somewhere, and both cars going out seven days a week translates into fourteen car-days per week. Each of those trips costs gas, and puts more wear-and-tear on our vehicles. Some countries and cities have made it the law to refrain from driving one day a week. You can—make your own pact not to drive your car one day a week. Leave it in the garage. If you love it so much you can't take your eyes off of it, wash it instead of driving it. Remember, staying home isn't such a bad thing, either—this "policy" will make that happen.

Practice natural flea control.

Ask your vet about flea control and he or she will happily sell you a $17-dollar monthly system. Ask someone who practices a more natural approach to caring for their pets and they will tell you to put garlic in their food. Brewer's yeast is also an inexpensive, non-toxic way to keep your pets flea-free.

Cats should not be given raw garlic as it can be toxic to them. Jennifer used to slip her dog garlic in a scrambled egg every so often and found that to work well. You can find out more inexpensive and non-toxic flea-control techniques at www.eartheasy.com.

Make your own cleaning supplies.

Instead of spending money at the grocery store on expensive household foaming cleaners, you can make your own simple and non-toxic cleanser by mixing equal parts baking soda and Borax. Shake a bit out, add a drop of dishwashing liquid, and scrub away. Jennifer's thrifty sister Anne swears by it and gave out boxes of the mixture as Christmas gifts for like-minded friends.

Cut down the cost of kids' parties.

When did it become so costly to throw your child a birthday party? One of the biggest costs is the "goody bag" that some party-going children have come to expect. These are bags of candy and small toys that the host gives to the party guests. What? It is time to draw the line and forget that habit ever existed. Each one of those bags can cost several dollars to fill.

Keep your credit record clean.

You know this already—by paying your bills on time you will ensure that you never have to pay expensive late fees or be subject to a dramatic rise in your interest rate triggered by late payments. There are other reasons to keep your credit record as squeaky clean as possible nowadays: it helps to determine the interest rate when you want to borrow money.

Employers are also taking credit records into account when considering who to hire. You don't want to lose a job possibility because of late fees or unpaid bills.

Find a per-mile auto policy.

Most car insurance companies look for ways to compete, and one way is offering people who drive less a preferred rate. Makes sense—if you drive less, there's less chance of an accident, right? See if your insurer or one of their subsidiaries offers such policies—unless, of course, you put 40,000 miles a year on your car. These policies work especially well if you have more cars than drivers, which might be the case if you have some kind of "leisure driving" or fun vehicle.

Keep a car two years longer.

Cars are expensive! And as most of you know, they depreciate more in the first few years you own them, especially if they are new. So we say that everyone should keep a car for an extra two years. If you typically drive a car for six years before replacing it, do this three times, and you'll buy one less car during the next twenty-four years. That's a big savings, which gets even bigger when you add in the sales taxes, value-driven registration fees, and higher insurance you won't be paying. These days, cars are made to last longer: They've worked out a lot of bugs, like susceptibility to rust and cheap carburetors that used to limit their lives. Keep yours in good shape, keep it clean so you like it more, and those extra two years will be a piece of cake!

Take a job for the employee discount.

You might already be working more than one job, but if you have the time and energy to add another one, choose it according to the kind of employee discount you get. If you have a major purchase in the future—a new carpet, say, or a large piece of furniture—why not look for a second job at a retailer who sells what you need. Employees frequently get up to a 40 percent discount, which can add up to big savings.

Peter worked several Christmas seasons for the national housewares chain, Restoration Hardware, and used his employee discount to save big on towels, rugs, and a large oak desk. He saved hundreds on those purchases.

If you find yourself with a shopping hobby you just can't give up, look for a job where the employee discount will take some of the sting out of what you spend. Book lovers can work in bookstores, coffee addicts can take a side job as a barista, and clothing lovers can work in a boutique.

Sleep naked.

You will never need to buy pajamas again!

Shower together. Save water.

Another sort of sexy way to save is to take short showers in the morning with your partner. You will spend less on hot water and use less water overall.

eating-out habits you might be able to
. Start earlier and take advantage of Early
..s or Happy Hours with free appetizers. Ask your
..rite restaurant if they have any early-bird specials, and
make sure you show up at the right time to get the best
price.

Be wary of coupons.

Coupons are popular again, but they aren't always a bargain
shopper's friend. Why not? Because armed with a coupon
for something you need and buy anyway, you can save. But,
dazzled by a coupon that will save money on something you
never buy and don't really need, you end up spending more
at the grocery store than had you not brought the coupon.

Carefully examine your own standard purchases. If you
can find coupons for these items, wonderful. Use them. But
don't let yourself be swayed into buying more than you
meant on things you don't need. You can find online sources
for coupons at www.centsoff.com. There is a fee to join, and
there is also a shipping fee for the coupons you order.

*"It's good to have money and the things that
money can buy, but it's good, too, to check up
once in a while and make sure that you haven't
lost the things that money can't buy."*

—George Horace Lorimer

Make your own baking mixes.

Marcie Rothman, the Five Dollar Chef, says that one of her biggest gripes about groceries is the amount shoppers spend on prepared mixes. "You can make your own flavored rice, or ground beef casserole for so much less. You don't need to buy Hamburger Helper."

You can learn how to make your own baking mixes at www.budget101.com/convenience_mixes.htm. The site gives a lengthy list of recipes for mixes, including ones for apple muffins, delicious puddings and cakes, and even Alfredo sauce.

Lose the "latte factor" and other money traps.

Financial advisor David Bach continues to point out the "latte factor" that keeps so many people from being able to get ahead financially. Spend $4 or $5 a day on lattes, and it quickly adds up to real money—money that could be invested, used to pay down debt, or added to a savings account.

But not everyone drinks a latte a day. You might, however, have some other unconscious habit that is also leaking money away from your savings account. Maybe the magazine you buy a few times a week to read at lunch? That also adds up quickly. A weekly manicure appointment? That might be money you can use elsewhere right now. Look around and see if you don't have a latte factor operating in your life.

Take a free outing.

There are so many ways to spend a pleasant afternoon outdoors that are absolutely free: bird-watching in a meadow, hiking on a mountainside, running next to a lake. Instead of a trip to the shopping mall or an afternoon at the movies, put on your walking shoes and go outside. It costs nothing, and might even pay some health rewards.

Back to the dorms to save money on the road.

Hotels can add up when you are traveling, particularly overseas. But hey, by reverting back to your youthful ways, you can save big by staying in college dorms. Yes, when dorm rooms are empty in the summer, many colleges rent them to travelers.

England is among the best places to stay in dorm rooms; there you can find rooms anywhere from $22 per person to over $100—far less than you'd pay to stay in a hotel.

For info on finding dorm rooms to rent, check out www .reidsguides.com.

"Money cannot buy peace of mind, greatness of spirit, serenity, confidence, or self-sufficiency."
—Plutarch

Clean your refrigerator coils.

If you've ever looked under or behind your refrigerator, you've probably seen those metal grates and tubes known as coils. Or maybe you haven't—because they're so covered with dirt and dust bunnies that they look more like forest floor than part of a kitchen appliance. If that's the case, you have an opportunity. Refrigerators (and freezers) circulate coolant through those coils to transfer heat out of the refrigerator and into the air around the unit. If they're dirty, they don't transfer that heat well, and your refrigerator has to work harder. That's more energy used and a trip to an appliance store sooner than you'd like. So get a coil brush at your hardware store, and have at it.

Clean your own carpet.

The carpet cleaner who regularly parks that van by your house will have to find something else to do, because you will soon be cleaning your own carpets. It isn't hard (in fact it is great exercise!), and it isn't expensive. Rent a carpet cleaner at your local hardware store or grocery store for around $20 for twenty-four hours. (Think how many rooms you can clean in that time!) Spend another $20 on the special soap used in the machine.

Compare that to the average of more than $100, and you can see why the guy or gal with the van might soon need to look for another line of work!

Stop drinking bottled water.

Bottled water? Who thought that one up anyway? You now routinely pay for something you get at home for free. . . . So stop doing it. Not only can you save money—$1 a bottle—but you will help turn back a big environmental scourge. Empty water bottles are everywhere!

If you have a hard time giving this habit up, perhaps this will convince you—both Coke and Pepsi (who own the big bottled-water labels) have admitted that their water comes from municipal water sources. Which means it is the same water that comes out of your tap. Fill up a hiking bottle with water from your own faucet and save.

Install a low-flow showerhead.

Ah, that nice, hot shower feels good, doesn't it? But even five minutes worth can use thirty gallons of water. If half of that shower water is hot, depending on your utility rates, your shower could burn 50 cents to $1 in hot water. And if you take a longer shower—more hot water, higher cost. Do it every day, and soon your water-heating dollars add up—right along with the cost of the water itself. Such showers may consume as much as 25 percent of the water used in your home. One answer is a low-flow showerhead, which is cheap at your hardware store and possibly free from your utility (never hurts to ask). A 2-gallon-per-minute (gpm) head might reduce water use by two-thirds, and it almost feels as good as a regular shower.

Make your own carpet freshener.

Why pay a few dollars for a spray or powder that makes your carpet smell good when you can easily make your own? Buy a big box of baking soda. Add some dried lavender seeds or finely chopped rosemary leaves. Pour it into an empty pizza cheese shaker, and there you have it—your own scented room freshener. Walk around the room shaking it everywhere, wait fifteen or so minutes, and vacuum it up. Just like the store-bought, but you made it yourself for less.

"What are three words that profile the affluent? Frugal, frugal, frugal."

—Thomas J. Stanley and William D. Danko

Make your own air freshener.

Like making your own carpet freshener, you can also easily make air freshener. Take an empty spray bottle and fill with distilled water. Add a few drops of your favorite essential oil to the water, and spritz away.

Watch those bank ATM fees.

You're out on a warm Friday evening, and wouldn't it be good to get an ice cream cone? Sure. Your family would love it. Only thing is, you're out of cash. But wait—you have your ATM card. Simply walk down the street to the Fifth National Bank and get $20; you're on your way. That's true, but it might cost you $3, $4, maybe more to get that money. Why? Because you're using an out-of-network ATM. They charge a fee (to help pay for the machine, etc.) and then your bank charges a fee (well...because they're your bank). It can really add up: The average out-of-network fee is $3.43. How to avoid this fee? Plan ahead, and use your own bank (stop on the way, don't wait to get there and have to backtrack) or try a credit union—many of these not-for-profit institutions pick up these charges for you. You can also get extra cash at the grocery store without paying extra.

"Money is a mirror. An examination of your money and the way you use money is a way of understanding yourself in the same way that a mirror provides a way of seeing yourself."

–Michael Phillips

Why not opt out?

Drum roll, please. The best way to save money is ... not to spend it. So much of what we spend our money on nowadays isn't essential. It can certainly feel essential, because years of exposure to advertising and commercials have made us feel that way. But if you stop and ask yourself—What is this really for? Why do I really need it? Can I just do without it altogether? The answer might well be yes. Yes, you can opt out of the buying cycle.

Jennifer's big sister Anne practices simple living in Chicago. Her method of examining every big purchase is this—wait. If there is something that one day you think you absolutely need, wait a day or two before you make the purchase. Let your feelings rest. Perhaps a day or two later you will still need to make that purchase. But it is also very likely that a day or two later the feeling will have passed, that what seemed so very essential at that moment now seems far less essential. So opt out and don't buy it.

Skip the gift wrap.

At Christmas, on birthdays, Mother's Day, Father's Day, we buy lots of paper—very pretty paper, but it is paper we don't really need. Go ahead and skip spending money on wrapping paper; the person receiving your gift won't notice for a moment, and it won't diminish the thought behind the gift. You can tell people you are going "green" if you want, and are skipping the wrapping because it is bad for the environment. Instead of buying a roll or several sheets of gift wrap, you might try a little creativity and use scraps of fabric that you already have, newspaper, or just a pretty ribbon.

Learn to love *ReadyMade*.

Not ready-made meals; we think they are too expensive. Not ready-made vacations; we think they are too expensive too. No, we mean *ReadyMade* magazine.

ReadyMade is filled with ideas on how to make things out of other things, thereby cutting down the cost of whatever it is you need. Like this—turn old skateboards into the headboard for a child's bed, folded cardboard into a backpack, or a broken umbrella into a magazine rack. Seriously.

Check out www.readymademag.com, and you will never again look at the things you own the same way! And in the future you won't have to spend money on anything, because you can make it out of something you've got lying around the house already.

Walk! Park your car and get some exercise.

The best way to stretch your gas money is to leave your car parked and walk instead. It is rumored that short trips of 1 mile or less are the number-one reason for most American car trips. And, according to the Web site www.walkscore.com, a study in Washington State found that the average resident of a pedestrian-friendly neighborhood weighs seven pounds less than someone who lives in a sprawling neighborhood.

So next time you think about climbing in your car to drive somewhere nearby, stop and think—can I walk there? Can I ride my bike? The life (and the money) you save may be your own.

Form a babysitting co-op.

If you live in a kid-packed neighborhood or have friends with children whose ages match yours, perhaps you can save each other money on babysitting by forming a co-op. How would that work? Simple. Everyone gets a night, or maybe an afternoon, to themselves when they drop their children off with you. When it is your night, you drop your kids off with them. Simple.

How much can you save? If you are gone for three hours, and would have spent $10 an hour on your teenaged babysitter, you just saved $30. Do it once a week and that is well over $100 you (and your fellow co-op friends) will save each month.

Save money on Oprah's clothes.

Jennifer loves designer consignment stores and looks for them in every city she visits. In Chicago, that means visiting Oprah's Closet in the back of the Oprah Store across from Oprah's Harpo Studios. The studio address is 1058 W. Washington Boulevard, Chicago.

Yes, you can own Oprah's clothes. Really fancy stuff, for far less than it costs to buy it new and you get to tell your friends—"This old thing? I got it from Oprah."

Skip the Christmas tree.

How much did you spend on a tree this year? $50? $100? Lots more? This year, go ahead and skip the tree.

Use your imagination. What if you just tied a few big pine branches together and put them in a big planter and decorated those? Decorate an indoor tree that you already have, or hang the fireplace mantel with twinkly lights and make that the focal place for gifts. There are plenty of ways to make your house feel festive and ready for a holiday without the big decorated tree.

Establish your own holiday traditions that are unique. No need to rush out and have a tree just because everyone else does, right?

Look for used and rebuilt appliances.

Buying stuff used always saves money, and unless you're trying to make a style statement with your washer and dryer or refrigerator, you might do well to buy used. Same for that freezer you want for your garage, so you can take advantage of bulk food prices at your local warehouse club. Most good-sized cities and towns have at least one dealer or a few enterprising individuals who specialize in reconditioning appliances. Check out Craigslist, too. Only one caveat—if the unit is too old or not a current design, it can use a lot more energy—look for an "Energy Star" rating or even better, the original EnergyGuide label.

Drink Prosecco instead of champagne.

Champagne is not cheap. Well, it can be cheap, but that is not the kind of champagne you want to be drinking—trust us on this. So rather than give up celebratory bubbly stuff altogether, try Prosecco instead.

Prosecco is Italian bubbly, and the Italians drink it all day long, sort of like Diet Pepsi. A very good bottle of Prosecco is less than $20, far cheaper than a very good bottle of champagne. See? Already you have another good reason to celebrate!

Learn to make soup.

Few things are as cozy and comforting as the smell of a pot of soup simmering on your stove. Cozy, comforting, and in most cases, cheap. Soups are a convenient and cost-effective way to use up leftovers, and can sometimes be made from what you already have in your cupboard or refrigerator. Mix up a big batch and freeze small individual portions to take to work for lunch, maximizing your savings.

If you keep a bag of potatoes and a few onions on hand, along with bags of frozen vegetables, cans of tomatoes (or your own homemade sauce from your new tomato crop!) you will always have the basics for soup. Using water instead of broth is the cheapest way to make soup, unless you have broth you made yourself from leftover chicken.

A good source of simple soup recipes is www.annies recipes.com.

Form a book-swap club.

Books can be expensive, and the library doesn't always have what you are looking for. Form a book swap group with your friends to keep new and interesting reads in circulation amongst yourselves.

Invite your reader friends over for coffee and encourage everyone to bring several books that they read and enjoyed and would be willing to swap away for something new to read. Everyone brings a few books, and everyone leaves with a few books. Happy readers for no cost at all!

If you'd rather swap with strangers, try www.book mooch.com, or www.paperbackswap.com.

Slow down for savings.

You may remember the national 55 miles per hour speed limit of years gone by, which was enacted at the height of the 1973–74 oil crisis. The government had a point: Driving slower saves gas. According to the EPA's fueleconomy .gov Web site, every 5 mph over 60 adds the equivalent of 20 cents per gallon to the price of your gas (by using more gas). Or, put another way, a car getting 30 miles per gallon at speeds of between 45 and 60 mph gets only 23 mpg at 70 mph. Big, big difference.

Carpool with your neighbors on short trips.

On your way out the door to the store? Why not stop next door and see if your neighbor needs to go to the grocery too. If you all develop the habit of checking with each other to see if you can form short, casual carpools for errands, everyone will save overall on the cost of gas. Enough shared rides can add up over time, and you will all feel good about doing something for the planet.

Try a volunteer vacation.

A good way to travel for less is to do a "volunteer vacation," a trip where the point isn't so much sightseeing and pleasure as it is a chance for you to get involved in a good cause and help out those who need it.

Habitat for Humanity is still working hard in the Gulf Coast region to rebuild after Hurricane Katrina. If you've always wanted to go to New Orleans but worry about the cost, this might be for you. Look on their Web site for information: www.habitat-nola.org.

You can find outdoors volunteer vacations at www.sierra club.org, or a broader range of choices at www.charityguide .org.

Some of a volunteer vacation might even be tax deductible. Check with the organization and your accountant.

e tours for free travel.

Are you a take-charge kind of person? If so, you might be able to travel for free. Many hotels and cruise lines will compensate one person who brings a large group. Here is what www .latitudeworldtours.com says about their offer: "When you have six or more travelers you can save significantly...even travel for free! When your group travels together on one of our scheduled departures you can receive the following savings:

- Twelve guests plus yourself, you can receive a 100 percent discount on the land portion of the program.
- Eight guests plus yourself, you can receive a 75 percent discount on the land portion of the program.
- Six guests plus yourself, you can receive a 50 percent discount on the land portion of the program.

Not too shabby. You can use the savings to travel yourself or share the savings and provide a discount for every member of your group. It is up to you.

Watch *The Story of Stuff.*

This will only take twenty minutes out of your day, but the impact on your spending habits will stay for a lifetime. Check it out this minute at www.storyofstuff.com. The producer, Annie Leonard, will walk you through how things are made, how things are used, and how things are thrown away. Never again will you casually buy something unnecessary after you become aware of the story behind so much of what we buy and consume. Watch it, and then send the link to everyone you know.

Lease your garden space to a small farmer.

Not up to planting a vegetable garden on your own property? Why not offer it to a gardener in exchange for either cash or free vegetables? Many small-space dwellers are envious of their lawn-laden friends and would jump at the chance to come and garden on your property. Put the word out that you would welcome another gardener on your property.

There is a new movement called SPIN farming (small space intensive) in which urban yards are being used for small farming plots. Learn more about it at www.spinfarming.com, perhaps you will want to put your own front yard to use.

"Buy land. They're not making it anymore."

—Will Rogers

Dump bagged salad.

Put that bag of salad back on the produce shelf and pick up a simple head of lettuce instead. Karen Shuppert, who blogs about healthy eating and cooking at www.cook4seasons.com, has this to say about the cost of bagged salad: "Washed and bagged greens can be a time-saver, but they can cost three times as much as buying the same amount as a head of lettuce. Even more expensive are "salad kits," where you get some greens, a small bag of dressing, and a small bag of croutons." Read that? Three times more expensive than buying a single head of lettuce.

before you buy.

We've been driving the same Ford Explorer for seventeen years, and have saved thousands on car depreciation, sales taxes, and registration fees along the way. Of course, that means fixing it once in a while, but the costs of these fixes pales in comparison to those expenses. The lesson here— make an attempt to fix things before you replace them. Lawnmower breaks? Computer goes dead? There are services that will fix these items (and some of you have "smart friends" who can do it too). That doesn't mean everything can or should be fixed, but it's worth a try before giving up.

Learn to be a handyperson.

So you are going to fix your old car, lawn mower, or computer before heading out to buy a new one, right? But what if you don't have the knowledge or a handy friend who does? Not to worry, go to www.doityourself.com and learn the skills you need to fix your own things.

Everything from installing an ornamental fence to unclogging a toilet to what is politely known as "household rodent control," can be learned in easy-to-understand language.

Skip the extended warranty.

Bought a new TV or appliance or home theater unit lately? Bet you got a lecture as you prepared to swipe your credit card—something about a protection plan? Sixty bucks for a three-year warranty on that $250 iPod, $120 for that $1,500 TV, maybe $1,500 for that $20,000 car. Sounds pretty good— we all like insurance, don't we? But be careful. First, know that the sales person, who might get a few bucks commission on the iPod sale, might get a 50 percent cut on the extended warranty sale. Hence the sales pitch.

That should tell you something about what the warranty is really worth. Take extended warranty offers with a grain of salt: 1) you should buy high enough quality to not need one, 2) the fine print about what they don't cover (like "cosmetic" damage) can kill you, and 3) what you'll pay for the warranty might pay for a major repair or a substantial portion of a replacement product anyway. And if you have to replace, you'll get the latest and greatest with zero miles on it.

Skip the middleman and sell it yourself.

You can sell your house without a realtor and save yourself thousands. You can find the simple steps to handle the marketing and actual legal transaction at www.forsalebyowner .com.

the middleman and buy it yourself.

Buy your own stocks online to reduce trading fees, buy a well-kept used car off of the lot at CarMax, buy the item you want directly from the manufacturer. Whenever you can, try to avoid situations in which commissioned sales people stand between you and what you want.

Get your art events free.

Joe Napoleon goes to the theater for free. He gets to see every big-deal play and musical that comes to San Francisco and even gets to peek behind the curtain at the action now and then. How does he make that happen? He is a volunteer usher at one of the major theaters in town.

Museum docents also get in free and are welcome at insider events. Many arts organizations have had to cut back on staff and would welcome volunteer office help in exchange for tickets. What is it that most makes your heart sing? Call the office that makes it happen and see if they need volunteers.

Go off-season for best value.

Have your heart set on a particular travel destination? Call and ask when the off-season is and find the cheapest time to travel. Even the Ritz-Carlton goes on sale. Its resort property in Half Moon Bay offers the lowest rates of the year mid-November through mid-March.

Use a gold card for coffee—and more.

Starbucks recently introduced a Gold Card of their very own. And like American Express's Gold Card, it will cost you to get it. Pay the $25 purchase price, though, and the best part is that in return you will get two hours of free wireless access every time you visit a Starbucks, and also save 10 percent on all of your purchases. Ten percent of a pound of coffee a week will quickly earn back your $25 investment and then save you more, and eliminating your wireless at home to sit in Starbucks for two hours a day will add up even faster.

Borrow a new bag.

Purses are essential; we know that. But purses can also run hundreds and even thousands of dollars. What is a budget-minded fashionista to do? Join Bag Borrow or Steal. www.bagborroworsteal.com introduced the fashion world to a unique concept a few years ago—that by becoming a member you could "rent" popular purses on a returnable basis. Rent the evening bag you need for a special night out, rent the impressive and serious-looking leather satchel for a job interview, rent the bag-of-the-moment that you just can't live without . . . until the next one comes along. Give up your purse-buying addiction and become a purse renter instead!

Check out these prices: If you feel the need to impress your friends on vacation with your fancy Vuitton luggage, rent the canvas keepall (retail price $1,220) for $250 a month. So much cheaper than buying it. Bag Borrow or Steal also sells used designer purses, sunglasses, and jewelry in their outlet section.

"The rich are dull and they drink too much."

—Ernest Hemingway

Drop towing insurance.

Insurance companies love to add extras to your auto policy; it makes the total tab seem cheaper while still helping them meet their revenue and profit targets. One of those extras is towing coverage. You may end up paying $10 to $20 per year extra—per vehicle—for this coverage. But you can get the same coverage from an AAA (Triple-A, or American Automobile Association) membership for roughly the same amount of dough, and you can get all those nice maps and other services, too.

Paint for a new look.

Jennifer gets tired of furniture easily, but instead of rushing out to buy new, she reaches for a paint can. A fresh color, and the world looks bright and shiny again. Buy old wooden chairs at garage sales, give them a quick coat of new color, and change the way your dining room looks. You'll spend far less than if you headed for the mall furniture store.

Travel for medical care.

If you're paying your own tab, or most of it, for medical or dental care, geography does make a difference. Suppose you live in Northern California and have relatives in Cincinnati, Ohio. You can combine a visit with medical work. According to health insurer Aetna, a cholesterol screening costing $61 in California is $21 in Cincinnati. An arthroscopic knee procedure is $6,300 vs. $7,100, and a sigmoidoscopy will cost hundreds less. Take the concept beyond U.S. borders: A dental crown costing $900 is $300 in Tijuana, Mexico, and a knee replacement costing over $40,000 is $9,000 in Singapore. Check out www.medicaltourism.com to learn more, or simply do a search on "Tijuana dentist" or a similar one suited to your more specific needs.

Read this book.

And then read this other book—*The Overspent American*, by Juliet B. Schor. It will open your eyes to the way we as a nation have lived for the past few decades. We've been working primarily to pay for our spending habits, you see. So if we cut back on our spending, much of the money anxiety and work anxiety goes away. Head down to your local library and spend a quiet afternoon with her ideas.

Don't shy away from silly names.

In our neighborhood there are stores called "Grocery Outlet" and "Stupid Prices." Hmmm . . . maybe the neighbors will talk if they see us heading that way. . . . Well, get over your qualms. Silly names for businesses, but pretty good prices inside. Both stores are mostly on the West coast, but there will be something similar near you. Abandon your concerns about "how it will look" for you to shop in a place you might not have gone to before, whether it is a thrift store, a day-old bread store, or a cut-rate grocery store outlet.

Cuddle up at night.

Lower your heat at night to save. Pile on the blankets, cuddle up, and remember to wear socks. Keeping your feet warm at night helps you fall asleep faster.

"Abundance will never be a factor of how much money one has. Rather it is always a factor of how one feels about what money one does have."

—Stuart Wilde

Share wireless with the neighbors.

Those wireless connections sure are strong—up to a few hundred feet depending on the equipment. So why then, should we all have our own in houses that are so close together? Wouldn't it make more sense from a cash perspective if you formed a neighborhood collective and pooled in to pay just one or two of those bills and cancelled the other accounts?

Are you overinsured?

If you have health insurance, you might be double insured for medical coverage on your auto insurance. Take a look at your auto policy and see if it makes sense to drop that part of your plan. Discuss it with your agent and find out what the implications are. On the other hand, if you have medical insurance with a high deductible, you might be better off keeping it.

Go outside to eat.

Picnic every chance you get. Toss a blanket down on the grass, pull out a humble sandwich, and suddenly, the world is a beautiful place. Bring your simple and inexpensive meal and get the natural atmosphere for free!

Plan an at-home spa day for yourself.

Skip the fancy spas altogether and plan an at-home spa day for yourself. Beauty products are not hard to make. You can give yourself an inexpensive scrub by combining the following: ½ cup grated citrus zest, ½ cup plain almonds, ⅓ cup sea salt, 1 tablespoon almond oil. Combine the zest and almonds in a blender, mix it up, then add the sea salt and the oil and stir well. Store in a glass jar. Now you can smooth your skin with your own homemade scrub.

You can make yourself a conditioning hair treatment like this: Combine 2 tablespoons almond oil with four drops citrus essential oil. Massage this mixture through your hair. Leave it in at least twenty minutes before shampooing.

Save money on simple legal matters.

Before you hire an attorney, check out the do-it-yourself legal books and forms published by Nolo Books at www .nolo.com, or check out www.legalzoom.com. LegalZoom helps you create reliable legal documents from your home or office. You can get help with legal documents like wills and trusts, partnership agreements, divorce, name changes, and more.

Save money on phone calls.

Remember when calling someone in another country was a huge big deal and a major expense? No longer. Check out Skype and learn how to make free PC-to-PC calls to people anywhere in the world. You can also make free video conferencing calls. Check it out at www.skype.com to see if it will work for you. The newly introduced Skype To Go number allows you to make Skype calls from a phone, rather than a computer.

Check out the movie matinee.

Remember this money saver—matinees. The first showing at many movie theaters around the country is usually several dollars less expensive than the regular ticket price. In fact, to address the current economy, movie theaters in the San Francisco Bay Area have actually dropped the price on their matinees. We hope this is happening in your part of the country too! Get back into the habit of seeing movies early in the day and paying less. Skip the popcorn and soda and you can get in and out for less than $7 in some places.

Increase your homeowners' or renters' deductibles.

The increase-the-deductibles theme occurs elsewhere among our 573 tips, and it's a good one. When you increase a deductible, you take on more exposure to the first few dollars of a claim, but you can save a heck of a lot on the insurance bill. You're rolling the dice a bit—hoping not to have a claim at all—but isn't it better to save a known chunk of money than to be covered for what might happen? We save about $700 a year by carrying a $5,000 deductible instead of a $1,000 deductible on our home. So if someone breaks the big picture window, well, we're on the hook. But if the house burns down or someone falls on the front steps, we still have good coverage, and it's nice not to pay $700 a year for $4,000 in insurance. After six years, we're ahead even if there is a claim.

"What can be measured can be understood. What can be understood can be altered."

—Katherine Neville

Is there a discount in your wallet?

You might already be carrying an extra discount in your wallet. It might be your AAA membership card (always ask for the AAA discount when making hotel reservations); it might be your AARP membership; or it might even be your Costco card. Jennifer's parents saved thousands of dollars on a car purchase because they were Costco members. "Any group memberships?" the salesperson asked them, "Any memberships at all?" Why yes, they had this one card here . . . and it did the trick.

Examine everything you already belong to and all those pieces of plastic you cart around every day, and see if there is an additional use you've lost track of. Check out the membership Web sites to see if there are new benefits you could be using.

Hot rocks at home.

Love those spa treatments with the warm river rocks soothing your sore aching muscles? You know, you can do something similar at home, for free.

Sesame oil makes an inexpensive massage oil. Add a drop or two of your favorite essential oil to give it some scent. Collect smooth medium-size rocks and clean them well. Jennifer warms her rocks in hot water and removes them with a large wooden spoon. Rub massage oil on your skin, and start moving your handful of warm rocks over the slippery surface. Works even better if someone else rubs for you. You can learn massage techniques to try on each other at www .wonderhowto.com, in the diet and health section.

Increase your health insurance deductibles.

Everyone knows about the crisis in health care costs, which rise 7 to 10 percent and sometimes more per year. It used to be that employer-provided health plans covered almost everything except perhaps the $5 co-pay for a doctor visit. Not any more. Higher co-pays—and deductibles—are the norm. Most likely you'll be offered several choices among health plans. You may find that you pay a lot out of pocket for your premiums to get that deductible down. We recently experienced a $2,400 annual drop in premiums by switching from a $4,800 family deductible to an $8,000 deductible in a health-savings-account-compatible high-deductible health plan. We were paying $2,400 a year for $3,200 of insurance coverage! Didn't make sense. Sit down with your benefits specialist or an agent, and make the right choice. You might be eligible for the health savings account, too.

Stargaze.

Every night there is a spectacular show you can enjoy for free. It is in the sky above you. Stargazing is a great way to spend an evening with your children, and it is both cost-free and educational. Spread out a blanket on the grass, lie down on your backs, and talk about what is in the sky. Meteor showers can be a good excuse to stay up late (strictly for scientific purposes, of course) to watch an even more exciting light show.

Make your own moth repellent.

Don't buy chemical moth repellent or moth balls; use natural methods for free instead. Moths dislike rosemary. If it grows in your garden, cut several small sprigs and hang it from a clothes hanger in your closet. If you don't have a ready source of rosemary in your own yard, look around the neighborhood to see who does. Knock on the door and ask your neighbor if you can cut a bunch. You can also use lavender, mint, thyme, and eucalyptus for the same effect.

Turn off your television.

This will save you money. Why? Because studies have shown that the more hours you spend watching TV, the greater the chance you will overspend. Think about it—you are exposing yourself over and over to advertisements. So turn your set off and, with it, turn off those constant nudges to buy stuff.

Don't buy too much life insurance.

Sure, it's nice to be insured against the worst possible calamities. If you die, you want to make sure your loved ones are protected with adequate resources at least until they can recover from your loss. But what if you don't have any dependents? What if your loved ones are independently wealthy or have a rich 95-year old uncle? Sure, financial security feels good, but why pay for insurance you don't need? Think about what really would happen if you died; then talk to an insurance agent. You might be better served with disability insurance, which you're two and a half times as likely to need.

Stop and smell the roses.

If you don't have a garden to relax in at home, take advantage of your town's public gardens. Pack a picnic lunch and set up near the roses, bring a book to read on a bench near a lake. Enjoy the sights, sounds, and smells of a well-maintained public space.

Pick fruit in your neighborhood.

"I looked out the window, and there was a woman with a plastic bag picking oranges off the tree!" Susan Carson told us. "A wealthy woman! I couldn't believe it." Everyone is out on the street looking for freebies nowadays, so we aren't surprised. What can you find? Well, you might find a neighbor's tree that no one is picking. Offer to pick it for them, and share the bounty. Oranges, lemons, grapefruits, apples, and pears—what are your neighbors growing that might be shared? Don't be shy in offering your time in harvesting fruit off of trees they may consider only ornamental.

Years ago Jennifer had a nighttime dog-walking ritual that took her down alleys where fruit trees grew over the fence. Most nights she came home with a little something for breakfast the next day.

Travel in your imagination.

You might not be able to hop a plane to Paris this year, but you can still travel there in your imagination. Or to Italy, Spain, Turkey, or whatever spot most appeals to you. Read novels set in the parts of the world that most intrigue you and soak up the atmosphere on the page. Perhaps you already have a CD of music that will match the mood (or check the library).

Make your own luxury bath oil.

Mmmm, expensive bath oil is so luxurious. But hey, so is the stuff you can make yourself for far less. Baby oil is the basic ingredient. A generic bottle costs little more than $1. To add a favorite smell, you can use a drop of your favorite perfume, or a drop or two of essential oils. Mix and store in a glass jar.

"The general foible of mankind is in the pursuit of wealth to no end."

—Benjamin Franklin

Try a Korean bathhouse.

If you live in a major city with a large Korean community, you can skip the pricey spa and head straight for a Korean bathhouse to indulge in a daylong communal experience for a very low price. Twenty dollars gets you a day pass to LA's Natura Sports Health Club, www.natura-spa.com. Jennifer's sister Anne describes her experience: "For $18 dollars I spend two hours at the Paradise Sauna in Chicago, the Korean bath in my neighborhood. I go back and forth between the dry sauna, the cold plunge, the steam room, and the Jacuzzi. I'm a limp rag by the end of it. On a cold winter night it is heaven."

Quit the gym and walk with your partner.

How much do you pay a month for your gym membership— $39? $49? More? And how often do you use it? If you aren't going in often enough to bring your per-visit cost down to less than $5 (if you pay $39 a month and go ten times, you are paying about four dollars a workout), then why not cancel the membership, keep the money, and get your exercise by walking for free? With your love. You can work on your body and your relationship at the same time.

Pack your lunch for the plane.

Remember the good old days, when airlines served food? It was tasteless, but gosh, it was free. Now they want $5 for this, $5 for that. Skip food fees on board and tote your own meals or snacks. Whether it is a humble PB&J sandwich or a more elaborate arrangement of fruit, cheese, and crackers, it will likely be better than what the flight attendant is selling and will cost you far less money.

Find last-minute bargain trips.

Sign up for one of the email alert services at www.travelzoo .com to hear about last-minute travel bargains. Also look at www.us.lastminute.com and www.lastminutetravel.com.

Read aloud to each other.

You read to your kids, of course you do, but why not read aloud to your love as well? It is a romantic and absolutely free way to spend an evening. Instead of a fancy dinner out, light candles, get cozy on the couch, and take turns reading a novel out loud to each other. You might want to wait until the kids are in bed to give this one a try.

Go back to school.

Adult learning centers, university extensions, and community classes are all bargain ways to learn new skills, explore new interests, and meet new friends. A small investment can bring big rewards. Find out what is going on in your community.

Listen for free.

Opera, theater, orchestral music, jazz, band music—all summer long in most communities you can hear music at free outdoor performances. Take advantage of what your town has to offer. Check with your local arts groups to find out what's planned, or call your local Chamber of Commerce for information. Become a student of the "What's Happening This Weekend" section of your local newspaper and keep on top of the free possibilities available to you and your family.

"Having money is rather like being a blonde. It is more fun but not vital."

—Mary Quant

Make your own gifts.

Instead of buying expensive gifts for family and friends, you can make your own meaningful gifts. Do you have crafting skills? Put them to use. Cooking skills? Homemade baked goods are always a hit. Do you garden? A freshly picked bouquet is a delightful present.

If you don't have the crafty talent it takes to make gifts, write out "personal promise cards." You remember how these work—promise to do the housework for someone, promise to pull weeds in the yard, promise to give a massage. Promise to do something that will put a smile on the face of the recipient. These make perfect gifts—no money required.

Keep your nails short.

In Jennifer's neighborhood a manicure costs $25. And that is the price for "natural nails." If you have acrylic nails get ready to spend even more on a very regular basis. That might have seemed possible a year or two ago, but for now, consider keeping your nails natural and short. Not having a regular manicure can add up to well over $100 in savings every few months. Go without, or get back in the habit of doing it yourself in front of the television.

Check your kilowatts.

As author Katherine Neville put it so well in her novel *The Eight*, "What can be measured can be understood; what can be understood can be altered." So say you want to save a little on your electric bill. A good place to start would be to know how much electricity is used by your TV, appliances, lights, and other electrical items in your home. The biggest users, of course, need the most attention: You should begin to consistently use those less or possibly even replace them. So now, how to measure? A small company called P3 International markets a device called "Kill A Watt," which records electricity usage for anything plugged into it (http://www.p3international.com/products/special/P4400/P4400-CE.html). Although it doesn't work for direct-wired devices like water heaters, it's a handy little device that can tell you more about what you use. If nothing else, it will help settle arguments about which things—or who—around the house uses the most juice.

Weatherstrip the house.

You've probably heard it a hundred times from your utility and read it a dozen times in various magazines. Weatherstrip your home to seal out drafts and keep the cold (and warm) outside where it belongs. It really does work and can save up to 15 percent of your home heating and cooling costs. It's easy too, and you'll have fewer drafts and be more comfortable. After you're done with the windows and doors, finish up with attic entrances, spaces around pipe entrances under sinks, and even wall switches and receptacles—these "leaks" can cost, too.

Buy in season. Eat in season.

Few things are as delicious or as good for yc
berries, so it's hard to resist picking up that
in the produce section of the store. But wait, what m...
is this? Unless it is smack in the middle of blueberry season,
keep walking.

The best prices (not to mention the best flavors) for
fresh fruits and vegetables are when the growing season is in
full swing. If you buy out of season you are paying too much
for something grown far away. Try to buy from local growers
if possible, at farmers markets. Towards the end of the day
you can get further bargains buying bruised fruit that vendors want to sell quickly.

Make your own tomato sauce.

Okay, write this down—five fresh tomatoes, some olive oil,
some garlic, some parsley, salt, and pepper. Think you can
handle that? Of course you can, and in ten minutes you will
have made a simple tomato sauce that is cheaper and better
for you than the sauce at the store. In the summer when
your neighbors and coworkers are looking around for people who want tomatoes, raise your hand high.

You can find a simple sauce recipe at www.101cookbooks
.com. Look for the Five Minute Tomato Sauce Recipe. It uses a
28oz can of tomatoes rather than fresh, though. For a sauce
recipe using fresh tomatoes, go to www.recipezaar.com.

Find a small hotel room.

What is the point of a large hotel room? For some trips you are hardly in the room at all except to sleep. So for those trips, seek out a hotel room with little more than a bed. Check out the Jane Hotel in New York, with ship-cabin-sized rooms and shared baths for $99. An even less expensive New York alternative is The Pod Hotel, with rooms as low as $69.

When traveling, find the store.

A bag of candy in the hotel minibar is what, $10? Okay, maybe not that much, but that day may be around the corner. Never take something from the minibar, and keep travel costs lower by looking for a grocery store near your hotel. Ask at the front desk about the nearest full-service grocery store and stock up on fruit, cereal, bagels, and your favorite soda.

Jennifer always makes it a point to buy soup mixes and then heat the water with the hotel room coffee pot. Her children expect to eat soup in coffee mugs in hotel rooms. Don't feel shy about asking room service or the restaurant for any spoons, knives, or forks you need.

Visit cities with good public transportation.

You find a great airfare, a bargain hotel room price, and then renting a car jacks up the price of your trip. So why not make it a point to vacation in cities with great public transportation and skip that cost. Everyone knows the famous ones—New York, Chicago, Paris, London—but don't overlook Honolulu. They have a great bus system that can take you all over the island without a car.

And although Los Angeles hasn't yet fully developed their Metro system to the point of greatness, there is a wonderful trolley system for the airport hotels. You can take the "Ocean Express Trolley" from many of the hotels near the airport to the beach town of Manhattan Beach and hang out on the beach all day.

Travel with your own bar.

This is a habit Jennifer picked up from her parents, who always brought a little something with them on family car trips and sat down for a civilized drink in a funky motel room while their children watched cartoons. Skip the drink or two in the hotel bar and instead pour one of your own for far less. This only works on road trips, of course; don't try to pack a bottle of liquor in your luggage on the plane. You can easily save $10 or $12 on your pre-dinner cocktails. Use that ice bucket and save!

Share subscriptions or swap magazines with friends.

How many magazines do you subscribe to? Two? Four? Eight? At $20 or $30 apiece, they add up to serious money. Ask friends with similar reading tastes if they'd like to share the price of a subscription. You can also agree in advance to swap the magazines you subscribe to with the ones they subscribe to. If you can't find anyone to share costs, stop in the library and see if it subscribes to your favorites.

Sign up for restaurant newsletters.

Does your favorite restaurant have an e-mail newsletter? Sign up if it does. Restaurants now regularly send out specials and discounts to their regular customers via e-mail, and you can receive a substantial discount sometimes. We got an offer from a local gourmet pizza house—buy a $50 gift card for only $32. A savings of $18! That is more than 30 percent. We did, of course.

Sign up, and you will soon receive offers for free desserts and appetizers, special holiday offerings, and insider info. Large national chains also have newsletters that regularly offer discounts. The upscale steak chain Morton's sends out e-mail specials several times a year. Check it out at www .mortons.com.

Make your own jewelry.

Just as making your own gifts is more fun and more meaningful, so too is making your own jewelry. Stay out of the mall jewelry stores; instead take a class in jewelry design, beading, or working with metal.

Have fruit for dessert.

Skip the heavy, caloric, and expensive cupcakes, cookies, pies, and chocolates for dessert and instead reach for a piece of fruit. You will feel better about yourself and be healthier in the long run.

BYOC—Bring your own coffee, that is.

So . . . how much do you spend on cups of coffee during the week? Spend one week's worth of coffee money on a nice insulated thermos and make a pot at home to bring to work instead of popping into the cafe on your way. Because it isn't just the coffee, it is also the scone, the muffin, and the croissant that begin to add up to serious money you could be saving for something else.

Make muffins for breakfast on the go.

Make your own muffins. They are one of the easiest things you can bake (from scratch, please—no mixes, which cost too much, and aren't healthy) and they freeze well. You can also use up bruised fruit like bananas, apples, and peaches. Make a batch of twelve and freeze some for your mornings on the go.

Good muffin recipes abound; look for them at www.eat betteramerica.com.

Drive across the country for free.

Need to get across the country but don't have a car right now? Rental cars are expensive. Maybe you can drive someone else's car.

Actually, you can. If you are older than twenty-three and have a good driving record, check with www.autodrive away.com to see what needs to be driven where. More than 20,000 people just like you do this every year. Pick up a car at the Auto Drive Away office (there are twenty scattered around the country) and drive off to the destination. The first tank of gas is provided; after that it is up to you to pay for gas. Likewise you have to pay for your meals and lodging. What you get is the use of someone else's car, for nothing.

Ride share on long trips.

So if you did get a car from Auto Drive Away, why not advertise where you are going and see if someone else needs to go there and split the cost of gas? Remember the "ride-share" board at college? Jennifer rode home from Portland to Sacramento many times in college with complete strangers—fellow students going in the same direction who wanted to split the cost.

Get back into the habit. Craigslist has a "rideshare" function, and check out the site at www.goodala.com. You type in where you are and where you want to go and see if anyone is offering to take riders along for gas money.

Learn to house swap.

Live in a major metropolitan area with lots of international cachet? If so, you might be able to vacation for free by trading homes with someone in an equally attractive destination. HomeLink International (www.homelink-usa.com) has been arranging house exchanges since 1953. It isn't free to use the service: Membership is $110 a year, but the raves on the site make it sound worthwhile. Think of what you would save in hotel costs by staying free in another country while that homeowner comes and stays at your house.

Learn to couch surf.

There is more than one way to stay for free. If you don't have a house to swap, do you have a couch someone could sleep on? Then check out www.couchsurf.com, a nonprofit organization with members all over the world who offer up their couches for free to other members. You could travel the world from couch to couch, sleeping for free and meeting interesting people in the process.

Start neighborhood potluck dinners.

Both money and time are saved when meals are shared. So why not organize a weekly potluck in your neighborhood? Rotate the house that hosts, and agree in advance about who will bring what kind of dish. Every Sunday night, or perhaps every Thursday night, families can get together for a group meal to solidify their community and lighten costs for everyone. It makes a perfect time too to arrange yard equipment swaps, pass on old ski equipment, or plan joint vacations in which the group splits the cost of a house, or ... The possibilities are endless. Build a greater sense of community and everyone will benefit.

Switch your games.

Are your children nagging you to buy the latest games and game platforms? Tell them to leave you alone, and to join www.switchgames.com instead. A self-described community that "supports the trading of games, consoles, and accessories, SwitchGames will let members trade games for free. Beats another trip to the mall.

Travel off season for best prices.

Visit a famous ski town in the summer, check out the desert in the winter, and go to the beach when everyone else has headed home. Many resorts are focused on making their money on one season only, and then just hanging on until that season rolls around again. So go visit when only the locals are there; you will spend far less—more than 50 percent in many cases—and get a better sense of what the community is really like. Not only will you save money, but in a place like the Hamptons on New York's Long Island, you won't have to fight for a parking place. You will be able to get a reservation at the trendy hot spots, and you won't have to deal with the summer traffic.

Buy a second home now?

For most, buying a second home would hardly be considered a way to save money. Of course, you end up with another mortgage, another property-tax bill, another set of utility bills, maintenance, and so forth. But if a second home has been on your wish list, and especially if it might provide you a path to downsize some day for retirement or for other reasons, now might be the time to look. Prices and interest rates are as attractive as ever. Even if you don't buy, it gives you something good to dream about, something to put the other 572 tips in this book in play to save for.

Wash your own car.

Go to the gas station, fill the tank, add $4 for the car wash, maybe more if you get one of those wax jobs you really don't need. Sure, it's convenient, and your car comes out looking a whole lot better. But it only takes care of the outside. What about the inside? If you use the car wash once a week for a year and throw in one of those hand washes and vacuum jobs for $20 every now and then, pretty soon you're into some real money, especially if you have more than one car. So we say, do it yourself. It isn't real hard work. It's one of those "pride of ownership" things, and the interior of your car will get cleaned more often, too. That's the part you see the most anyway.

Get the lead out—of your trunk.

Your car's trunk is a handy place to store all sorts of things—car stuff, sports stuff, that return-bound bag of cement you never used for that fencepost project. Whatever it is, it adds up, and every one hundred pounds removed can improve fuel economy by 2 percent, according to a Federal Trade Commission report.

Plan a "staycation."

Why not save money, time, and beat the crowds by planning a "staycation" this year. Go ahead and take the time off work like you usually do, but use this as an opportunity to be a tourist in your own town. Visit all of the places you keep meaning to go—the museum, the old part of town, your childhood haunts. You could also use it as down time to catch up on house projects. Just don't overload yourself too much. Remember, this is your vacation, even if you never leave your property this year.

Go for organic grocery deals.

Organic food does have a reputation for being expensive, but if you are committed to this type of healthful eating you should visit Organic Grocery Deals, www.organicgrocery deals.com. Dedicated to helping "our members save money on their quest of going organic," the site offers blog posts and discussion threads about what is on sale at Whole Foods and other big chains and where to find coupons for organic products.

Use cloth napkins.

Drop paper napkins from your standard grocery list and instead, start to use the cloth napkins you have in a drawer. Don't save them for company; use them for your own every-day needs. It is better for the environment in the long run, and in the short run will both save money and remind you at your dinner table that everything should be used more than once. Wash them only every few days (encourage family members to refold them after use and leave them at their assigned place at the table).

Use your hanky.

See above.

Mix your own stuff from concentrate.

Convenience is king these days. Want to buy orange juice? Simply head to the refrigerated aisle and pick up a half gallon or gallon already premixed. Need Roundup weed killer? Simply buy one of those one-gallon premixed jugs, complete with sprayer attached. Here's the rub—you pay for that convenience, as much as twice as much. And besides, if we're talking Roundup, if you mix your own, you can make it a bit stronger to get rid of those really big weeds.

Switch to compact fluorescent bu

They're showing up pretty much everywhere—
curly-Q fluorescent light bulbs. Yes, they're more
to buy than their traditional incandescent counterparts, but
they'll save a lot in the long run. Typical indoor bulbs save
about two-thirds of the energy per equivalent light unit, and
they'll last four to five times as long. And now even those
outdoor floodlights have fluorescent versions. Spend a little
more now; save a lot later.

Cut back on laundry soap.

Peter worked at the test labs of a major soap manufacturer,
so he has a good grasp on how things get cleaned. Most of
us use too much soap when doing a load of laundry. Read
the side of the box and make sure you are not overfilling the
measuring cup, it can be very hard to find the filler line sometimes. Jennifer believes that, unless you are digging ditches
for a living, you can get away with using a little less soap to
clean your clothes than the box actually recommends. Use a
tad less, and your soap will last a tad longer.

"Make all you can, save all you can, give all
you can."

—John Wesley

Las Vegas on sale!

"What happens in Vegas, stays in Vegas," the commercials promised us all recently. What has happened in Vegas lately, though, is that not as many people stay there. If the idea of visiting Las Vegas has always appealed to you, this is an ideal time to do it. Rooms, food, and entertainment are marked down. Even the world-famous Cirque de Soleil has had to offer specially reduced prices. Hang on to your wallet in the casinos, though; gambling is never a way to save money.

Take a road trip!

Pile the family in the car and see the country instead of flying over it. Planning a family road trip can be a fun and less expensive alternative to flying to a vacation destination. Get creative and plan a theme like "U.S. history" or "best road-side burger" and seek out low-cost motels instead of full-service hotels.

Buy at factory outlets.

Like that really cool JBL bookshelf or computer speaker system? Check out the Harman International factory Web site (www.harman.com)—you can get remanufactured units sometimes for 50 percent off. This works well for computers and other kinds of manufactured goods—just go to the manufacturer's Web site and look for the outlet store. Plenty of bargains, and you might save on sales tax, too.

Buy an almost-new car instead.

According to the Kelley Blue Book (www.kbb.com), the average car loses about 65 percent of its value in the first five years of ownership. Some cars lose as much as 35 percent of their value in the first year of ownership. So how do you save money on cars? Buy them when they're a few years old. If you want to find a lot of relatively late-model used cars in the "sweet spot" on this depreciation curve, and don't want to trust and haggle with dealers or private parties, try used car "automotive superstore" CarMax (www.carmax.com). They specialize in selling exactly the cars you might be looking for.

Doublecheck your ISP.

The Internet has happened fast, and most of us have jumped on board. As fast as the Internet is evolving, you might expect your own Internet service provider to evolve, too. Most of us started out with dial-up and moved to broadband—if that's you, check and see if you're still paying that old dial-up bill. If you don't need it, chuck it. And many of those old broadband deals included equipment rental charges—which were set to go way up after a one-year teaser period. If you're paying $40 or $50 a month for Internet service, there's probably a better alternative, including buying your own equipment and paying a technician to install it.

Never dial 411.

Time was when you could call your telephone information service, or even your operator, to get a phone number cheap and easy—maybe for 50 cents. Well, in today's competitive world, phone companies have lowered their prices but kept several "revenue enhancers" around—like information services. Nowadays you might pay $1.50, maybe more, for cellular information services. Okay, if it's an emergency, fine. But if you're just out to see if your favorite restaurant has a table for two tonight, let your fingers do the walking, or better yet, use your search engine. And if you have data service on your cell phone, do a search on that. Store your important phone numbers in your phone, too.

Start a community garden patch.

Not everyone has the space to plant a full-fledged vegetable garden, and not everyone has the time to weed. Gather your closest neighbors together and see if you can't come up with a community garden plan that works for everyone. You can pool money to buy seeds; pool efforts to clear, plant, and weed; and even better, pool the results for delicious fresh meals you can all enjoy. It may be that one neighbor has the space to lend, one neighbor has the cash to buy seed, one neighbor has the time and energy to keep it weeded, and one neighbor knows how to can so you can all enjoy your produce all year long.

Buying car insurance? Get all the discounts.

Car insurance is expensive; we all know that. And most of the insurers know that too. So they've dreamed up all kinds of discounts off their "rack rate" to stay competitive and attract the "right" kinds of customers. You can get discounts if you own multiple cars or insure your home with the same insurer. Most people know that teens with driver training or good grades get discounts. But did you know that some insurers give discounts for drivers of hybrid vehicles? For members of professional organizations? Discounts for over-50 or nonsmokers or cars with ABS brakes? Sit down with your agent and go through the possibilities—you might save 25 percent or more on your insurance.

Use your cell phone for long distance.

Time was when a long-distance phone call was a real luxury, when even a short call could cost $10 or $15. Those days have gone by. Long-distance service has become competitive and cheap. But even if you're a modest user, it still may run you $20 to $30 or more a month. If you have a cell phone with nationwide coverage, use it for your long-distance calls, especially on nights and weekends when most minutes are free. You'll have to figure out the tradeoff—minutes used versus long-distance dollars saved—for the weekdays, but if you manage your minutes well, you should come out ahead.

Turn out the lights!

Much is made of saving energy by using compact fluorescent bulbs, energy-efficient appliances, and so forth. But it isn't just the rate at which you use energy, it's whether you use it at all that counts! Buying an energy-efficient bulb putting out 75 watts of light with 23 watts is nice, but what if you just turn out the lights instead? You'll save more. Get in the habit of turning out all lights except the ones immediately needed—and get the family in the habit too. It will save now—and in the future.

Delight in beans and rice.

Time to make friends with beans and rice. Even if you have a family of dedicated meat-lovers, everyone enjoys a good pot of beans. You can find good beans and rice recipes at www .vegetarian.about.com. You'll save money, and eating more beans and rice has nice health benefits too.

"There was a time when a fool and his money were soon parted, but now it happens to everybody."

—Adlai E. Stevenson

Pop real popcorn.

Want popcorn that tastes like popcorn and costs less? Then skip those microwave packages and reach instead for the old-fashioned popcorn in a plastic bag or glass jar. It costs less, you can make as much or as little as you want, and you can also flavor it any way you want. Use real butter, add cinnamon and sugar, go wild with your flavorings.

If you don't remember how to make it on the stove the old school way, there is a handy video on www.viewdo.com, search for How to Make Popcorn on the Stove.

Shop your pantry first.

Before you head to the store for a few things for dinner, why not stop by your pantry first to see if you can make a meal out of what you already have. Kids are always happy to have breakfast for dinner, so cereal and fruit are all you need. Kids will also eat lunch for dinner, so soup and sandwiches will work! Is there an old box of something in the back that needs to be used? Pasta and a can of sauce back there? Use up what you have before buying more.

...ine, that is.

...special-occasion dinner you will want to celebrate ...th a special bottle of wine. The most cost-effective way is to bring your own to the restaurant and pay their corkage fee. Corkage usually runs between $15 and $25. Why pay so much to bring your own bottle—one you might have already paid $30 for? Do the math: Restaurants mark their wine up between two and two-and-a-half times retail. So even if you bought a good bottle at a wine store for $50 and paid the restaurant $25 for the privilege of drinking your wonderful stuff, it is still better than buying the $75-bottle on their wine list. Why? Because it isn't really a $75-dollar bottle; it is a $30-bottle they have marked up considerably. Whereas you, you clever thing, are drinking a better bottle by far.

Check your grocery store's Web site.

Even if you are not a regular coupon clipper, you should get into the habit of checking your local grocery store's Web site on a regular basis. Jennifer just checked our local store's site as she was writing this—and found that by printing out a special coupon she could save $20 off $100 worth of purchases between Wednesday and Saturday. Sign up for your store's newsletter to get any special promotions or alerts.

Make a shopping list and stick to it.

To avoid impulse buys in the grocery store, always prepare a list in advance and stick to it. Don't let yourself be distracted by end-cap displays and in-store promotions. And remember the old rule about not shopping on an empty stomach, as you will end up buying more.

Form a buying club.

Annie Hope Malki in Miami was unhappy with the high cost of organic produce and thought if she could round up enough Floridians interested in organic, she could form a regional buying club. So she put up a Facebook group called Annie's Organic Buying Club. "My goal is to get organic produce for our members for 30 percent less." You can join Annie's Facebook group, or find more info on the Web site she created at www.anniesbuyingclub.com. You can also use Annie's method to organize your own buying club for people in your area. The more you buy, the better the price, so get others to join in with you.

"Acquaintance: A person whom we know well enough to borrow from, but not well enough to lend to."

—Ambrose Bierce

Don't toss out old bananas.

Make banana bread from the oldest, yuckiest bananas you have. Older bananas actually make more flavorful banana bread. The minute your kids turn up their noses at the bananas you have on hand—"Ewww, it has spots!"—you know you have what it takes to make a delicious treat for breakfast. For a good simple banana bread recipe, try www .foodnetwork.com.

Compare before you click the "buy" button.

When buying online from your favorite Web site, don't forget to price compare. Before you hit "buy," go to one of the comparison sites like www.pricegrabber.com to make sure you have found the best price.

"Given the choice between living prudently (and sleeping soundly at night) and squandering all your resources in an endless cycle of consumption and debt, which sounds like the better idea?"

—Peter and Jennifer Sander

Increase your auto insurance deductibles.

Most auto policies have a deductible amount for collision (if you wreck your car) and comprehensive (if someone else wrecks it for you, if it's damaged by storms, if it's stolen, if the windshield breaks, etc.). Those deductibles might be $125, $250, even $500 for the collision side. When bad stuff happens, it's nice to have a lower deductible, but at what price? You might pay $80 a year to keep a deductible at $250 instead of $500—that's $80 a year for $250's worth of insurance. Is that a good deal? Probably not. Get all the options from your agent, and don't pay top dollar for those first few dollars of coverage.

Ask: Is this a "want" or a "need?"

Of course you need that cashmere sweater. Of course you need that magazine. Or do you? Have a conversation with yourself about what are your "wants" versus your "needs." Remember that your needs are pretty basic—food, shelter, warmth.

"I have learnt to seek my happiness in limiting my desires, rather than attempting to satisfy them."

—John Stuart Mill

Say "no thanks" to cash.

It's become so easy to get extra cash, anytime, anywhere these days. Those of you old enough may remember the only way to get cash was to go to a bank and stand in line—when it happened to be open. That gave way to anytime, anywhere ATMs; today, you can get cash at the grocery, at the warehouse club, fast food joint, heck, even at the post office. But here's the problem—that extra twenty here, an extra twenty there can really add up. And those twenties tend to disappear fast once they find their way into your wallet. Here's how to save: budget your pocket cash and do it once a week at an ATM. Period. No extras, nowhere, no how.

Limit your family trips to the drive-thru lane.

You're running late, soccer practice just ended, and the kids need to get started on homework, so a quick run through Mickey D's looks like the best solution for everyone. Not really. Save money by packing sandwiches and snacks from home to eat in a situation like this.

"If money is your hope in independency you will never have it. The only real security that a man will have in this world is a reserve of knowledge, experience, and ability."

—Henry Ford

Never shop out of boredom.

So . . . nothing else going on today, might as well go to the mall. Spending time wandering around a mall because you have nothing better to do is certain to accomplish one of two things: increase the chances that you will spend money on something you can't afford, or increase the chances you'll become depressed about not being able to buy what you can't afford.

"Money is a singular thing. It ranks with love as man's greatest source of joy. And with death as his greatest source of anxiety."

—John Kenneth Galbraith

Don't go to the mall for exercise.

Lots of folks have convinced themselves that the best place to go and walk in the morning is in a local mall. It's big, it's warm, it's dry, and it's safe. Yes, it is all of those things. But it is also a daily opportunity to spend money, from the minute you buy a cup of coffee to the moment you once again look in the window of the dress shop and think about how cute that jacket it. You are exposing yourself to many money temptations daily, so why not just buy a warm rain jacket, find a walking buddy, and plan another route in the outdoors. This might well be the best way for seniors to walk, but if you have other options, find another routine.

Rank priority before you buy.

Just as you reach for an item, ask yourself—what is the priority? Is this a high-priority purchase, something that you or your family need to survive? Is it a medium priority, something you need but not to survive? Or is it a low priority? Low-priority things you can go ahead and skip for the most part. Asking yourself to rank priorities helps you keep bargain-busting items to a minimum.

Wait before you buy.

Jennifer's big sister Anne has a firm policy about large purchases—she waits a few days before she acts on her decision. Look at new television sets, decide on just which one you want, and then go home. Go home and let the idea settle for a bit. The overwhelming feeling of necessity might fade. You might decide to make do with what you have. Or, you might decide after a few days that you have made the right decision and go ahead with the purchase. If so, at least you won't beat yourself up for spending money impulsively.

"If you can, you will quickly find that the greatest rate of return you will earn is on your own personal spending. Being a smart shopper is the first step to getting rich."

—Mark Cuban

Lose weight.

Slim and active people are healthier. They pay less for health insurance; they spend less at the doctor. Their food bills are lower as they don't spend money on expensive snack food from the grocery store or meals at the local fast food outlet. Save money by cutting back on how much you eat and reap the health and financial benefits!

Cut back on cable.

Is it time to cut back to the cheapest cable package and forgo all of the extra channels? Hold a family meeting and see if your family will agree to go basic. They might surprise you and be willing to give it up altogether.

Find a store that doubles coupons.

Coupons can help you save money on the things you planned to buy anyway, and you can save even more when the value of the coupon is doubled. Large chains like Ralph's, Von's, and Safeway occasionally offer double-coupon days; ask at your local store. Type "double coupons grocery stores" into your search engine and see if you can find one near you. But remember—don't get suckered into buying something you don't need just because you have a coupon.

Use Facebook discount information.

Paulette Strauss started the Friends & Family Discount group on Facebook last fall because she was receiving so many e-mails with friends-and-family discount codes. "They were starting to clog up my inbox, so I thought it would be great to have them all in one place. I invited forty of my friends to join the group, and two months later over 1,000 people had signed on. The feedback I have received from people who post on the page is that they love that all of the discounts are easily accessible. And they wouldn't have known about some of the offers without seeing them on the Friends & Family Discount page." If you are a Facebook member, seek out the group and join.

Borrow a glittery gown.

Been invited to a fancy event but find yourself without enough cash to get a new glamour outfit? The perfect reason to rummage through a friend's closet. No one needs to know that is not your dress you are wearing. This is the reason you have friends, remember? So you can borrow their clothes.

Rent a glittery gown.

If you and your friends don't wear the same sizes, here is a bargain alternative to dropping big dough on an outfit—rent one. Just as men have always been able to rent formal wear, now women can too. Check out One Night Affair, www.one nightaffair.com.

Wash Fido and Fluffy yourself.

Few things bring you a greater feeling of closeness with your pets than hosing them down and soaping them up. Granted, there might have been a good reason that you were willing to pay someone else to do this task the past few years, but it is time to get back into the habit.

"A bank is a place that will lend you money if you can prove you don't need it."

—Bob Hope

Time for only one car?

Most American couples are two-car couples. Is it time to rethink that at your house? You might not bring your auto costs down by half, but your savings will be considerable. Taxes, insurance, gasoline, parking, repairs—think of it.

Instead of each of you driving around in your own car, can you give one up and commute together? Can one person work from home? Take public transportation? Bicycle? Don't approach it as a punishment for the one giving up a car; approach it as an opportunity to rethink your habits and decide that you can do things differently from now on.

"Auto insurance is a toll bridge, over which every honest driver has to pass."

—Jane Bryant Quinn

What exactly are you buying?

The next time you are about to buy something, stop and ask yourself—"What exactly am I buying here?" You might think you are buying an object, but many times what we are actually trying to buy is power, prestige, personal identity, or even love. Spencer Sherman of *The Cure for Money Madness* recommends stopping to take a "money breath" to examine what our real motives are. Once you recognize that you are not really buying a thing, but rather are buying a way to feel better, you might be able to relax and let the mood pass.

Rent instead of owning a home.

For years, federal government policy has been directed at making us all owners of the American dream. This policy succeeded to the tune of some 70 percent of American families owning a home by 2007. The trouble is, not all these families could afford their homes, as we painfully found out in the subsequent real estate bust. In fact, home prices were so high that annual rents, as a percentage of home prices, languished below 3 percent in many markets—that is, $18,000 a year, or $1,500 a month, might rent you a home priced over $600,000. That didn't make much sense to real estate investors, but it does point to the fact that sometimes renting is better, and in many markets today it continues to be less expensive in the long run to rent than to buy, even with the tax advantages of buying.

Professor and author Richard Florida also points to the advantage of having more flexibility as a renter; you can move to a better job on a moment's notice. With these thoughts in mind, run the numbers before deciding that you must own a home.

Change your driving route to avoid impulse buying.

Does your ordinary commute take you by places that you long to stop and shop in? Time to choose a different route. Redesign your driving patterns to avoid stores and restaurants that tempt you, and you will not have to grip the steering wheel every time you pass by.

Listen to Reverend Billy.

He isn't really a man of the cloth. In fact, Reverend Billy is here to convince you that you don't really need any more cloth. Or more anything, really. That you, we, all of us, have enough. And that we are headed for a Shopacollapse!

With a heavy dose of humor and some terrific acting, the performance actor Reverend Billy will get you thinking twice about consumption, credit card debt, and big box stores. You can find his videos on YouTube or at www.revbilly.com.

"The safe way to double your money is to fold it over once and put it in your pocket."

—Frank Hubbard

Keep what you own to go green.

Everyday a new product appears to help us go green. Should you rush out to buy it because, if you don't, you are harming the planet? No. Think about it—in many cases the greenest decision is to continue to use the things we already own, rather than buy something new to replace them. Don't feel guilty about using old appliances, non-organic sheets, books on non-recycled paper. Keep what you have, keep using it, and know that you are doing your part.

Ride your bike to save three ways.

You know that riding a bike instead of driving a car is a cheaper way to get from point A to point B, but there is more to it than that. In fact, riding a bicycle helps you save money in three different ways: You save on gasoline and auto wear and tear, you save on gym fees as you exercise for free, and you save on health care costs because you are slimmer and in better shape.

Airbed and breakfast.

Another very inexpensive way to travel is through www.air bedandbreakfast.com, where ordinary folks will rent you a room in their private home or apartment. Check out the site and see if you can skip the hotel costs on your next trip.

Serve smaller portions.

A standard dinner plate used to be 9 inches across. Know what it is now? Twelve inches. Our plates have grown along with our portions, and our waistlines. Cut costs by getting back to the smaller portions at mealtimes. Even using 10 percent less will stretch your meals further. You will have enough for a brown bag lunch the following day.

Make your own notepads and scratch paper.

Jennifer likes to gather the subscription cards out of magazines and staple them together to make small notepads—free and green. Cut up leftover paper that still has one side unused to make small notepads or scratch paper. Anytime you can save money and the planet at the same time it's a good thing.

Know that manufacturers are cutting sizes.

First there was super sizing—everything became really huge, from drinks to burgers to bags of popcorn. But now you need to pay close attention because things are shrinking on the retail shelf. "Short sizing" is the term for it, and it is what happens when the price of your favorite tub of ice cream is the same, but you sense that something is different. It is this: The package is smaller. Many food manufacturers are keeping their prices the same for products—everything from peanut butter to mayonnaise to cereal—but are shrinking the size of the package it comes in.

To stay abreast of this and make sure you are getting your money's worth, pay close attention to the per-unit price. Put on your reading glasses and squint at that small tag on the shelf; it will tell you the per unit price.

Be "frucall."

Yes, you are trying to be frugal. When you are out shopping you can also be "frucall." The free comparison-shopping site at www.frucall.com allows members to text in the barcode of an item and get a text back with the lowest price the site finds. This gives you the knowledge you need to either cut a better deal or walk away.

Always ask, "What specials are you offering today?"

Memorize this phrase, and use it everywhere—when you sit down to have a haircut, when you are scanning a menu, when you are considering a piece of clothing in a boutique. Maybe there really is a special that day, or maybe if you are asking nicely enough, the person in charge might just make one up for you.

Always search the words "discount" and "sale."

No matter what you are looking for, and no matter how well you think you know the price, it always pays to go online and, in your search engine, type in what you want along with the words "discount" or "sale."

Create low-cost organizers.

Stay out of the expensive organizing stores and instead use some of those shoe boxes you've been saving up for years. Cover them with contact paper, leftover wrapping paper, or scraps of fabric. Stack them on their sides or use them with lids to organize small things in your closet and have a more streamlined look.

Wash in cold water.

Fully 90 percent of the energy used by a washing machine (and hence the cost of the energy you used) is used to heat the water. So, use cold water. Unless you are washing really soiled clothing, most ordinary dirt will come out with a cold-water wash. You can add to the cold-water cleaning power by loading up the washing machine in the morning with clothes, soap, and water, and then stop the cycle so that it soaks all day long. When you are back from work, start the rest of the cycle.

"There were times my pants were so thin I could sit on a dime and tell if it was heads or tails."

—Spencer Tracy

Skip the Spam.

Spam the meat—that is what we want you to skip. "This drives me crazy," Marcie Rothman, the Five Dollar Chef told us. "You don't have to eat Spam to save money. It is expensive on a per-ounce basis, and it is filled with sodium. You can do much better by just paying attention to the grocery store's meat specials."

Avoid the flu.

No one wants to get sick. You will miss work, you will feel lousy, you will have to stock up on expensive over-the-counter remedies. Consider avoiding all of those things by getting a flu shot. Many pharmacies now offer inexpensive flu shots and FluMist nasal immunization. You can find pharmacies near you that carry FluMist at www.flumist.com.

Skip the sugary cereals.

This is one of Jennifer's pet peeves, the high cost (and low nutritional value) of sugary cereals. Save money; buy oatmeal. Plain old homely oatmeal is good for you, inexpensive, and, if you really crave something sugary, tastes terrific with a bit of brown sugar added. Starting the day off with a warm bowl of oatmeal will make your whole world look better. Jennifer promises.

Make your own cheese.

Making bread seemed doable, tomato sauce and pizza you could handle—but cheese? Can you really make your own cheese at home? In fact, you can easily make one of the most expensive cheeses around, ricotta. Rather than spend the $7 at her local grocery store for a small tub of ricotta, Jennifer makes it several times a year. Spread fresh homemade ricotta on crostini (small toasted bread) and you have an impressive (but inexpensive) appetizer for guests.

Ricotta cheese requires just a few ingredients—a gallon of milk, some heavy cream, and some cheesecloth to strain it. You can find a simple recipe at www.saveur.com.

Whiten your own teeth.

Instead of having your dentist or hygienist whiten your teeth, lessen the cost by using the kits you can purchase at the drugstore. After all, the main ingredient is the same. "Peroxide is peroxide," one expert pointed out recently.

"Money in the bank is like toothpaste in the tube. Easy to take out, hard to put back."

—Earl Wilson

Try not to procrastinate.

"Never put off for tomorrow what you can do today" is a terrific money-saving slogan you should take to heart. Why? Because, in many cases, dragging your feet on a money-related issue can cost you money. If you procrastinate paying your bills, you will get hit by late-payment fees and higher interest rates. If you procrastinate in booking a flight, you will have to pay more than had you done it earlier. If you procrastinate when fixing an appliance, it might become unrepairable. If you procrastinate on a health issue, your condition could worsen and cost more to treat. And so on. So whatever needs to be done in your life, get on it now.

"How strange it is, that a fool or knave, with riches, should be treated with more respect by the world, than a good man, or a wise man in poverty!"

—Ann Radcliffe

Check out designer sales.

If you still have a shopping habit, try to stick to the discount sites for high fashion like www.bluefly.com and www.gilt.com. Gilt has a waiting list for membership, so put your name on it now and with luck you can be a member by the time you need to buy something wild.

Be a "budget fashionista."

Run by a dedicated blogger who wants to help women look fabulous on a budget, this site is filled with info on sales and coupons, discounts, and great deals: www.thebudgetfashionista .com.

Make your own fertilizer.

Get in the habit of composting your vegetable and garden scraps. You will do something nice for the planet, put less into the waste stream, and get free fertilizer for your garden in the process! You can find information on building your own compost bin at www.bluegrassgardens.com.

Don't waste a good recession.

We are living in interesting times. Rather than gripe about what has befallen us, use it as an opportunity to learn new things, gain new skills, and adopt a new approach to life. Focus on what is truly important to you, and let go of the things that were only superficial.

This is a unique chance to acquire the courage and discipline to make important changes that will serve you well in the long run.

Bring a friend to increase negotiation power.

Need to buy a car? Maybe your friend does too. Imagine how much more price flexibility you might achieve if you two could say to the car salesman (or refrigerator salesperson, or sofa saleswoman) "We are buying two of this. What can you do for us on the price?"

Enjoy the comfort of soup and a sandwich.

Rocky times call for comfort food, and few things are as comforting as a grilled cheese sandwich and a bowl of creamy tomato soup. It makes a perfect, and perfectly inexpensive, dinner meal at the end of a tough day. Feels like your mom is in the kitchen taking care of you (and telling you not to spend your money).

Cut the price you pay for haircuts.

To save money on haircuts for you and your children, look into being a hair model at your local salon (ask your beauty operator; she or he will know what you mean) or find a beauty school near you. Experienced students about to graduate are available to give haircuts and color for bargain prices.

Visit artists' studios.

If collecting art is your thing, check out open studio sales where you can deal directly with the artists themselves instead of with galleries. Your local community arts council might put together an annual art tour with a map that leads you on a leisurely afternoon drive from studio to studio. Many artists are selling at below-gallery prices (as they get to skip the gallery commission) and you can find some real bargains this way.

You might also be able to interest an artist in a trade for what you do—swap services or products. Chances are they are also short of cash nowadays and would be open to more flexible arrangements.

"Too many people spend money they haven't earned, to buy things they don't want, to impress people they don't like."

—Will Smith

Don't try to keep up with the Joneses.

Move past the idea that what you own tells people who you are. Give up the notion that your neighbors will think less of you if you don't have the same kind of fancy car in your driveway that they do. Trying to compete with other people in terms of image and prestige is always a losing game.

Avoid these premade items at grocery store.

Energy or protein bars should be crossed off you.
list. If you need a boost in the afternoon, buy plain almo..
and dried fruit instead. Energy bars are really just pricey
candy bars.

You can make your own spice mixes; you don't need
to buy them in a package. Before you buy any high-priced
spice mix just check your cupboard and see if you can mix
something similar with what you already own. Chances are
you have spices and dried herbs on the shelf that you haven't
used in years, so try to figure out a recipe in which you can
put them to use.

You can also make flavored rice dishes yourself without
overpaying for a small box of rice and a handful of salt and
herbs.

And finally, don't overpay for hamburger meat by buying preformed hamburger patties. Make them yourself and
freeze if you want to save a step, but don't pay more to have
someone else do it for you.

"It's not your salary that makes you rich, it's
your spending habits."

—Charles Jaffe

Hide your roots.

Women spend a lot of money on hair. Jennifer counts it as one of her biggest expenses and is always looking for new ways to reduce hair care costs. So if you have colored or highlighted hair, how can you stretch the weeks between appointments? By fixing your roots yourself.

Clairol's Nice and Easy Root Touch Up kit and other, similar products that you can use for temporary fixes are available at drugstores.

Cut it in half.

There are several beauty products that can be made to last longer (and therefore cost less per use) if you cut them in half. Pretreated facial cleansing pads can be cut in half, so can acne wipes that teens use. When tubes of beauty products seem empty, take a pair of scissors and cut off the bottom and squeeze those last few drops out the back end too.

Stay in the bar.

A great way to enjoy a night out in a restaurant and still stay on budget is to eat in the bar. Many nice restaurants have less expensive bar menus. Famed steakhouse chain Morton's has small hamburgers on their bar menu. You can still get dressed up and enjoy the restaurant's hospitality and atmosphere without facing the big dinner bill at the end of the evening.

Hostel environments can be good for your budget.

Remember those days as a carefree backpacker, staying in cheap student hostels? Hostels are still around, and you can still stay in them, even with children. Look for hostels with private rooms, like Santa Barbara's Hostel, www.sbhostel.com, a block from the beach. At $69 for a private room it is far less expensive and far more interesting than motel chain lodging. The Banana Bungalows, www.bananabungalow.com, are in Waikiki, Hollywood, and other fun destinations, and have inexpensive private rooms available for non-international travelers.

Be a buzz agent.

Sign up at www.bzzagent.com and become a "buzz agent." A company devoted to word-of-mouth marketing and "buzzing" its clients' products, BzzAgent uses volunteer agents who talk about products and places and receive discount coupons and free samples in return. Recent campaigns involved Boston Market and Chili's restaurants, as well as consumer products like dish soap and orange juice. Jennifer has done it for years and even got a free child's cell phone once.

Get the top twenty deals.

Sign up at www.travelzoo.com to get their weekly e-mail blast of the top twenty travel deals. These are generally last-minute offers on airline and hotel packages that sell at a substantial discount off the regular price. Even if you aren't in the mood to travel, some great deal just might convince you to pack a bag and go.

Try a McMassage.

No, McDonald's isn't really giving massages, but several large chains across the country are marketing massages like low-priced hamburgers. Massage Envy offers an introductory rate of $39 for a fifty-minute massage, a price that is hard to pass up. They have 500 outlets across the country. Look on their Web site, www.massageenvy.com, for one near you. There are similar, smaller chains: Look on their sites to see if they have a place near you: www.handandstone.com, www.massage heights.com, and www.zenmassageusa.com.

"I finally know what distinguishes man from other beasts: financial worries."

—Jules Renard

Time for cosmetic surgery?

Oddly enough, this is a great time to seek out price reductions on cosmetic surgery. Why? Because all of those folks who were getting Botox are starting to go without, and the popularity of elective procedures is falling. Plastic surgeons and dermatologists are not nearly as busy as they were last year, so you as a patient—probably a cash-paying patient—are in a very strong position. If you've always wanted to have a little something done, ask around and see who offers a good price. Make sure they all know you are asking more than one doctor for a quote, and that price matters.

Agree to let go of gifts.

Couples who are trying to rein in spending can have a serious talk about gift exchange. Instead of birthday-anniversary-Christmas-Valentine's Day-Mother's Day-Father's Day gifts, why not decide to forgo presents for a while, and instead focus on time spent together? Celebrate milestones and important events with a picnic, a long walk in the woods, a quiet evening on a blanket under the stars. Make each other cards and exchange promises to do things for each other.

Take up house-sitting.

For house-sitting opportunities, check out www.caretaker .org and sabbaticalhomes.com. You might be able to find a way to live without paying rent for a short period of time. *The Caretaker Gazette* sends subscribers information about caretaking and house-sitting positions, and you can also place "situation wanted" ads advertising your availability to house-sit or caretake.

Buy Christmas throughout the year.

Rather than wait until the last minute and buy too much for too much money, pick up a few things for Christmas gifts throughout the year. This will not only let you find interesting things at great prices, but it will keep you home and out of the malls at the moment you are most likely to overspend.

Be smart.

Are you smart enough to be a Mensa member? If so, join, as membership brings with it a number of cost-saving discounts and benefits: 20 percent off Choice Hotels, many reduced rates for magazine subscriptions, and savings on things like auto insurance, pet insurance, car rentals, and more. Check it out at www.us.mensa.org.

Cruise free.

Cruise ships invite talented professionals and authors to come along on cruises and give talks to passengers. In exchange, you cruise free. Sound like fun? Wine expert Roxanne Langer has done it many times, and is ready to go back for more: "My husband and I traveled on a cruise that would have cost $3,000 each. I gave five talks and relaxed onboard the rest of the time." Check out these booking agencies: www.sixthstar.com, www.toseawithz.com. Speakers do pay an administrative fee to book their cruise.

Switch to dial-up?

Dial-up. How old school. Yes, but also—how much less expensive. The recession has rekindled an interest in dial-up Internet service and companies like EarthLink and Net Zero are both marketing inexpensive dial-up plans for less than $10 a month. Compare that to the average U.S. broadband bill of $34.50 a month. If you don't really need hyperspeed at home, consider giving it up.

Watch your lead foot.

Stomp on that gas pedal, take off, beat the guy next to you. Feels good, right? Well, only until you start thinking about your hard-earned dollars fluttering out your tailpipe. According to the EPA's fueleconomy.gov Web site, so-called "aggressive driving"—that is, speeding, rapid acceleration, and braking—wastes gas. It can lower your gas mileage by 33 percent at highway speeds and by 5 percent around town. And it's not just about burning money; it's about making your car last longer, and it's about safety too.

Put on that sweater.

Drop the heat down a few more degrees and put on a warmer sweater. Cuddle up on the couch under a warm blanket. Remember to turn the heat down several degrees when you are going out for the evening. Even just a few percentage points can really make a difference on your overall heating bills. The U.S. Department of Energy suggests you can save around 10 percent a year on your heating and cooling bills by simply turning your thermostat back ten to fifteen degrees for eight hours.

Use cost-saving adoption strategies.

Odd to think about ways to save money when adopting, but expert author Laura-Lynne Powell shared the following ideas that could help families considering adoption right now: "Foreign adoption is the most expensive, so stay with a domestic adoption. Sign up with the state; it is less expensive than going private, but also means much longer waiting lists. Couples might also sign up with church-oriented groups. Let everyone know you want to adopt, they might hear of a birth mother looking for a family."

"Midas's Law: Possession diminishes perception of value, immediately."

—John Updike

Renovating? Try architectural salvage.

Need windows, doors, light fixtures? Check out www.redo .org to find an architectural salvage "ReStore" near you. When buildings are demolished, many elements are saved and can be purchased. Habitat for Humanity frequently receives donations from builders and homeowners and runs many of the architectural salvage operations around the country. Before you go to Home Depot and buy new, check into ReStores.

Yesterday's bread isn't bad.

Day-old bread stores hold great bargains and shouldn't be overlooked. If you don't think it is fresh enough for your tastes in a sandwich, then use it for breakfast toast, for bread puddings, stuffings, and toasted sandwiches. Keep some in your freezer for those purposes too. At bakeries, always look for yesterday's baked goodies, which are far cheaper and just as delicious when heated.

Don't shop at "discount" drug stores.

You know the places—Long's Drugs, Rite-Aid, Walgreens, Osco. One on every corner these days, perhaps, and they're hard to avoid, because sooner or later you need suntan lotion, Band-Aids, dog food, or milk, and you just don't feel like contending with a grocery or a big retailer. Sure, they're convenient. But despite the advertising, don't ever think they're cheap. In fact, if you take a close look at the pricing, you'll find they're more expensive than most places, including the grocery. That doesn't mean they don't have good "loss leader" deals once in a while, and it doesn't mean that convenience isn't worth something. But if you think of these stores as a big-box 7-Eleven you're on the right track.

Look for multiticket discounts.

When times are tough, people that sell entertainment and recreation suffer too, and one way they deal with that is to try to capture your loyalty, i.e., your return trip. So you'll see a lot more offers for multiple-visit discounts, like three-day skiing passes (three days for $49 each versus $69 a day at one near us). Look for multiticket offers on greens fees for golf, mini-packages of sports events or concerts by the local orchestra. These are often the best deals, since you get a discount but aren't committed to going every time. Some multiticket offers include parking and food discounts too. If there's something you've wanted to do for a while, check for specials on the Web.

Buy used rental equipment.

Looking for a snowboard or golf equipment or perhaps a power gardening tool? Check out rental places. Especially for sporting goods, rental places roll their inventory every few years, and think about it—each individual item doesn't really get much use, and it's only seasonal use anyway. So you can pick up some pretty good deals. Watch your local rental shops for deals, and if you don't see any, ask.

Nearsighted? Consider LASIK.

LASIK (laser-assisted in situ keratomileusis) reshapes your cornea to correct vision problems, namely nearsightedness and/or astigmatism. It's kind of expensive at perhaps $1,600 to $2,000 for a full treatment. Some might not like the idea of cutting the corneal flap, but it really isn't so bad (Peter's had it done) and there are now less invasive ways to do it. Anyway, that's not the point—the point is you get to save on all those glasses and contact lens replacements over the years, not to mention contact lens solutions and the like. As you age, you'll still need reading glasses, but you can get the simple drugstore versions. So over the years, you're likely to save a bundle. Have an optometrist or LASIK specialist run the numbers for you.

Buy less expensive sunglasses.

People spend gobs of money on fancy RayBans and Oakleys, only to lose them or have them sat on by children or ruined through any number of tough fates. The $15 and $20 varieties found in a common retail store or grocery are almost as good and offer the UV protection of the more expensive varieties. Better yet, you can afford to keep pairs in more than one place (like each car), so you're always prepared. Think about it—your eyes may actually get more protection this way than with the more expensive ones.

Look for secondhand season tickets.

If you crave sports but can't seem to find the tickets, and don't want to lay out thousands for season tickets (not to mention the time) there are ever more ways to climb on board at a reduced price. It's become easy to find individual or blocks of tickets on Craigslist, or check out Stubhub (www.stubhub.com) to get something closer to exactly what you want. This works for other things besides sports—such as concerts, performing arts, etc. You'll find it's a win-win—someone else has too many tickets (maybe their company bought them) or just plain can't go. Check it out.

Look for a cheap barber.

Guys (and some of you gals, too)—you don't have to spend $30 on a haircut and make an appointment a month in advance. The walk-in barber is making a comeback; sure, every small town has had its independent barbers for years. But for those in modern suburban America, where those independent guys are fewer and farther between, check out the various sports-themed shops, like "Champ Cuts," and get a simple buzz cut (any length you want)—it's often under $10, and they shave your neck hair, too. You can afford that clean-cut look more often than you think. Feels nice.

Get eye and other exams at a local university.

If you happen to live near a major university with a medical school, it's often possible to get routine exams, like eye exams, for cheap or even free at the school. And if not a major university, maybe there's a cooking school or a hair-styling school in your area. Check for bargains, and help a student learn.

Use flexible spending accounts.

Flexible spending accounts allow most employees to set aside pretax funds for medical and child-care expenses, thus saving payroll, federal, and state income taxes. That's a pretty good deal. You can use the health FSA funds for dentists, optometrists, glasses, prescription drugs, LASIK, and a variety of items you might not normally associate with "health care." Check with your benefits administrator. If you're self-employed or work in small business, a health savings account can accomplish much the same thing.

Buy a used bike—from the police?

Thousands of bikes are stolen each year—and guess what? Most of them are recovered. But unfortunately, since most bikes aren't licensed, the owners never find out. So police departments, overloaded with unused bicycles, sometimes sell them at rock-bottom prices. According to studies cited by the National Bike Registry, some 48 percent of stolen bikes are eventually recovered by law enforcement, but only 5 percent ever find their way back to the owners. So contact your local law enforcement agency or watch for sales. And if you don't want this to happen to your own bike, come up with a means to identify it, like putting a business card under the handlebar grip.

Use that wrap and ribbon again.

Keep wrapping paper out of the garbage and reduce your need to buy it by carefully smoothing it out and folding it up to use it again. Do the same with ribbons and bows and gift bags.

"The waste of money cures itself, for soon there is no more to waste."

—M. W. Harrison

Send Christmas postcards.

Do you still have that big stack of elegant Christmas cards you received from friends and family last year? Why not use them to make holiday postcards to send out next season? Just cut off the front part of the card (the part with the lovely artwork) and turn it into a postcard. Add a hand written message, which is so much more meaningful than a printed holiday message anyway. Best of all—postcard stamps are cheaper than regular stamps!

Take advantage of free fragrance.

Every women's magazine comes with a free bonus—those perfume strips tucked inside. Use them to scent your underwear drawer. Keep them in your purse to rub on your wrist before going out at night. Open one and tuck it between the seats in your car to give it a girly scent.

Make your own smoothies.

Get out of the habit of expensive fruit juice smoothies and get into the habit of making them yourself at home. Bananas, berries, ice, yogurt, juice, and a blender are all you need. Visit www.smoothieweb.com for a great selection of smoothie recipes.

Exercise more. Analyze less.

Studies have shown that a mere three hours of exercise every week has serious benefits not only for your body, but also for your mind and your mood. That is all the exercise it takes to make a significant difference in overcoming mild depression. Maybe you can run right past your therapist's office and wave.

Attend silent auctions.

Silent auctions at charity events can be a way to save money on luxuries, but they can easily be a way to spend too much. If there is something that you want, and if you know what the full retail value of the item is, decide what your bidding limit will be. Will you stop bidding if it goes more than 50 percent of the value? Or will you stop at 75 percent? Write down your bid and check it frequently before the bidding period closes, but do exercise restraint. Let someone else pay exactly what it is worth; you are on the prowl for bargains.

Jennifer has purchased many restaurant meals and ski lift tickets for far below the full price at charity auctions. Bottles of wine can also be had at a real bargain. Don't lose track of how much the item is really worth, though. Many auction attendees wake up the next morning with buyer's remorse at how much they spent.

Split a 12-inch sub.

A 12-inch sub sandwich for $5? Amazing. All the more amazing if you have two people with modest appetites who can each eat a 6-inch sub for lunch. Hope they leave that promotion running all year long at Subway!

Give each other foot massages.

If you are feeling deprived of luxurious spa services, learn how to give a foot massage. Yes, you can give yourself a foot massage, but it is even better if two of you learn how to do it, and give them to each other. All you need is massage lotion or oil. Check out the video on www.wonderhowto .com, under "foot massage."

Read the Bible free.

Free Bibles are available through Bibles for America at www .biblesforamerica.org, or by calling 1-800-551-0102.

"Empty pockets never held anyone back. It's only empty heads and empty hearts that do."

—Norman Vincent Peale

Get free samples.

Walmart's Web site has a section where you can get free samples of some products sent to you through the mail. Go to the "in stores now" section, and scroll down to "free sample." The selections are always changing, and take from four to six weeks to arrive by mail.

Get help with medical travel.

The Air Charity Network, www.aircharitynetwork.org, helps those in economic need who are in need of emergency medical transportation. Volunteer pilots around the country donate their time, their planes, and their fuel to make this possible. If you or a family member truly cannot afford to fly somewhere for medically necessary treatment, check into this organization.

Check your free credit report.

Every year you are legally entitled to receive a free copy of your credit report from the three credit agencies—Equifax, Experian, and Transunion. Staying on top of your credit report is critical, so take advantage of this service offered at www.experian.com, www.transunion.com, and www.equifax.com.

What's in the alley?

Jennifer's big sister Anne is an expert Chicago alley scavenger. She regularly walks her dog in the alleyways around her neighborhood and has found many useful furniture items over the years. "If it is set out in the alley, that is the universal sign that it is free for anyone who wants to haul it away," she says. The same is true of items set out on the street in other cities. Learn to paint and refinish wood and you will be amazed at what you can do with something no one else wanted.

Learn to say "no" to your children.

It's tough—we know that—but we all need to say "no" to our children more often. If your children have grown up in a more affluent time in your life, they might be surprised when you deny something they ask for. But by taking them into your confidence (in an age-appropriate way—don't tell them more than they can handle) about what is going in the world, they will quickly rise to the challenge. Don't feel guilty if you can't afford to buy them what they want, and don't get yourself into financial trouble because you can't say no.

Splurge in your bathroom.

If you feel the need to do something new in your house, sprucing up your bathroom can be done without too much expense. We don't mean new fixtures and lighting, we mean a new scented candle, some new hand towels, and a dish filled with sea shells from a recent vacation. Changing the look in small ways will give you a big boost without the big bills.

Buy new underwear instead of a new outfit.

Another small way to spruce things up is with new underwear. Skip the impulse to go out to the mall and buy a new outfit. If you really feel the need for something new to wear, buy some nice underpants and a new bra.

"Life shouldn't be printed on dollar bills."

—Clifford Odets

Get a free makeover.

The makeup counters at large department stores will help you look glamorous for free. Sit down and indulge in a free makeover. They do want you to buy their products, of course; that is why they are willing to do this. But if you have nerves of steel and can be impervious to lipstick and eyeliner suggestions, go ahead and get the makeover. Jennifer likes to bring in her cosmetics (from the same line as they are pushing) and ask them to teach her how to do something new with what she already has. That way she doesn't feel nearly as guilty about not buying something new, as it is clear that she has been a customer before.

"He that is of the opinion money will do everything may well be suspected of doing everything for money."

—Benjamin Franklin

Acquire some free peace of mind.

Learn to meditate. It is free, you can do it anywhere, and it will help you get through this part of your life. Read about some techniques you can try at www.learn-to-meditate.com.

Scent your fires.

Make your own scented fire starters by collecting small pine-cones, eucalyptus leaves, and dried herbs. Wrap them loosely in newspaper and add to your logs. Use sparingly. Jennifer also makes fire starters out of the trimmings from her lavender plants. Roll them up very tightly in small bundles and tie with thread.

Skip the take-out. Try a slow cooker.

If your rushed evening schedule is what sends you through the fast-food lane at the end of the day, why not start dinner in the morning and take care of the problem early? Use a slow cooker set to low to simmer stews and roasts all day long while you are gone. You will come home to a house that smells good, a healthy meal that costs less, and the knowledge that you are organized and efficient. Aren't you clever? You are also budget-minded, as slow cooking cheaper cuts of meat makes them tender.

"We can tell our values by looking at our check-book stubs."

—Gloria Steinem

Low income? Take advantage of lifeline service.

If your income is low enough, you might qualify for a "lifeline" rate from your local telephone service. Here is what the FCC has to say about it: Telephone service is considered a necessity for daily modern life. Yet the cost of starting and maintaining such service may be too high for some consumers. Under Congressional mandate, the federal Universal Service Fund (USF) supports the Lifeline Assistance and Link-Up America programs. These programs provide discounts on basic monthly service and initial installation or activation fees for telephone service at the primary residence to income-eligible consumers. The Federal Communications Commission (FCC), with the help of the Universal Service Administrative Company (USAC), administers the USF. For more information, visit www.lifelinesupport.org or call your local carrier.

Get help with energy costs from LIHEAP.

If your income is low enough, you might be able to get help paying your home energy bills. According to the Office of Community Services of the U.S. Department of Health and Human Services, the mission of the Low Income Home Energy Assistance Program (LIHEAP) is to assist low-income households, particularly those with the lowest incomes that pay a high proportion of household income for home energy, primarily in meeting their immediate home energy needs. The funds are administered by each individual state, and you can find your state's contact info by going to www.acf.hhs .gov/programs/ocs/liheap/grantees/states.html.

Eat free ice cream!

Every year for many years, the Ben & Jerry's ice cream store chain has held a Free Cone Day in the month of April. Check with the Ben & Jerry's closest to you to find out when the next one will be held.

Set your water heater lower.

Water heaters use energy "24x7x365," and in so doing account for about 13 percent of a household's utility expenses. According to the Department of Energy, if you lower your water heater setting from 150 degrees to 120 degrees, you could reduce its energy demand by up to 15 percent—and that can add up to as much as $50 or $75 a year if you live in an area with high utility costs. Combine that with using less and insulating hot water pipes, and you'll save even more.

Splurge on Sunday brunch.

We all love to relax in a beautiful restaurant, and it is hard to give that habit up. So, instead of costly dinners out, why not scale back and visit your favorite restaurant for an elegant Sunday brunch instead. The prices will be far lower, the pace much more stately than at a rushed lunchtime, and you will be happier when the bill comes.

Stock up on the Sunday paper.

For the price of your Sunday paper you get a big insert full of coupons. If they are the coupons that you use on a regular basis (remember, don't buy things you don't need just because you have a coupon for them), then why not invest in a second copy of the paper? If you are saving considerably more than the two dollars for a second copy, it could make sense. Even better would be to find a neighbor who takes the paper, but doesn't use their coupons.

Check out restaurant.com.

For those nights when you do head to a restaurant, try to find one in your area that has coupons available on www .restaurant.com. You can buy $25 certificates for as little as $10. Type your zip code into their site search function to see which restaurants near you are part of the program.

"Money is like a sixth sense without which you cannot make a complete use of the other five."

—W. Somerset Maugham

Bake your own Irish soda bread.

Now that you are eating more soup-based meals, go ahead and expand your bread choices too. A simple bread to make is Irish soda bread. It doesn't require yeast, kneading, or rising. A warm loaf of Irish soda bread along with butter and jam is a great weekend afternoon or after-school treat. The ingredients are plain, probably found in your cupboard: flour, oats, butter, and baking soda are the primary ones. It only takes twenty minutes (remember, no need for dough to rise).

You can find a recipe for Amazingly Easy Irish Soda Bread at www.allrecipes.com.

Make your own salad dressings.

Instead of spending several dollars on a bottle of expensive and high-calorie salad dressing, reach into your own cupboard for the simple ingredients you need to make your own. Olive oil and vinegar, along with salt and pepper, makes the most simple dressing of all. If you like the cheesy creamy kind, go ahead and add some blue cheese or other soft cheeses to the oil and vinegar mixture. The taste is better, the price is better, and it is a healthier choice —no preservatives, less sodium, and little fat.

Serve wine in small glasses.

Event planner Ingrid Lundquist taught us this trick: "If you are trying to cut down on your wine costs at a party, just use a smaller glass. Serve your guests in an eight-ounce glass instead of the big ten- or twelve-ounce goblets." It also works for your own dinner table; pour yourself a smaller serving in a smaller glass and have the bottle last an extra night without feeling deprived.

Skip the flower centerpiece.

One last piece of advice from Ingrid Lundquist—skip the expensive flower centerpiece and instead use interesting glassware to create a visual. She decorated one party table with the favorite objects of the host. You could even put a stack of your favorite books in the center of the table and use them as conversation starters. Who needs flowers?

"My problem lies in reconciling my gross habits with my net income."

—Errol Flynn

Make your own gourmet pizza.

It is easy to avoid the high-priced pizza in restaurants and the fancy stuff in the frozen case at the store if you learn how to make pizza dough yourself. A simple recipe for Quick Pizza Dough is found on www.foodnetwork.com. You can watch a video on www.monkeysee.com that will walk you through making your own pizza.

Invite your friends over to join you and see who can bring the most creative pizza topping. You provide the dough and the oven; they can bring along all manner of cheeses and meats and gourmet touches.

Try some Depression cooking with Clara.

Ninety-three-year-old Clara grew up during the Depression era and vividly remembers how her mother used simple and cheap ingredients to make satisfying meals. This is a skill that once again comes in handy, so watch the YouTube videos that Clara's younger relatives have made. She will show you how to make "Pasta and Peas," a dish she says her own mother made several times a week. Watching Clara move around her kitchen will also remind you that life is long, and that this too shall pass.

Don't rent a car at the airport.

Sure, it's handy—get off the plane, grab your bags, and head to the car rental counter (or even better, drive straight away if you're on the rental company's preferred customer list). Only thing is, you might pay through the roof. Car rental companies, particularly at airport locations, have become world class "unbundlers"; that is, they unbundle all sorts of costs out of the car-rental price and you end up paying extra fees—"passenger facility use charge," "shuttle charge," "airport tax" and so forth. Of course these are fees that any business would consider ordinary overhead—but here and now, you get hit with them. And of course, they're "catering" to business travelers, who usually don't care. Here's what to do—rent at an "off-airport" location. Enterprise Rent-a-car specializes in these, but there are others. And the good news: Most of them will pick you up, too.

"He is rich or poor according to what he is, not according to what he has."

—Henry Ward Beecher

Watch those hotel fees.

Following the lead of car-rental companies, hotels have gotten into the act of "unbundling"—that is, separating certain charges from the main room charge to make the room charge look more competitive. For years we've seen mini-bar charges, and for many years before cell phones, we saw irksome and outrageous phone charges, often pumped up by a "computer error" (how many times have we heard that one, and always in their favor, not ours?). Now it's parking fees, "resort fees," fees for use of exercise facilities, and so forth. Ask lots of questions before you book the room, and again when you check in. And take a close look at your bill when you check out, too.

Get nostalgic at a drive-in movie.

Is there still a drive-in movie theater near you? If so, load the kids in the car and go. Many outdoor movie theaters still charge by the car load instead of by the person, or they charge only adults and admit children under twelve free. Jennifer loads her car up in the summer with her children and their friends, brings along store-bought candy instead of expensive concession-stand fare, and can return home that evening having spent only $6 for her own admission. Such a deal. Check out the searchable database at www.drive-ins .com to see what is nearby.

Establish limits for birthday party gifts.

It's late Saturday morning, and Suzy needs to be at a party by 12:00 noon, and Joey needs to be at a friend's party at 2:00, and you don't have gifts or cards for either kid to take. No worries. Don't waste time and money in the toy store aisle trying to figure out who likes what. Establish a dollar limit with your children for their friend's birthday gifts—we say $20 per birthday party with ours—and buy gift cards from large stores like Target or Game Stop. For the birthday card itself, we insist our children make their own and skip the pricey store-bought cards.

Don't take your children to the store.

If you can avoid taking your children with you to a grocery store or on any kind of shopping outing, do it. Shopping without children in tow is less stressful time-wise, and you will avoid those scenes where otherwise sweet children cause a scene that only ends when you give in and buy them what they want.

If you use the birthday party method from the tip above, you can pick up the gift card yourself without having any children along on a toy-shopping excursion. It really cuts down on extra purchases.

Look up, look down, to spot bargains.

Grocery stores are minefields of tantalizing goodies, all displayed at eye level for maximum appeal. So, outwit them by not looking at the eye-level shelves, but rather at the top shelf and the bottom shelf to spot the best prices on the kinds of goods you need. The soup cans in the middle shelves will be higher priced than the ones you have to look up and reach for, or bend down and pick up.

Be wary of rebates.

Rebates are a terrific way to make a purchase look more affordable, but the truth is that the companies count on the fact that not everyone actually pursues the rebate. Don't be one of those people. If you buy something because there is an attractive rebate, hang on to the receipts you need, get the form you need (ask the clerk if you don't get anything automatically), and send it right away as there can be a time limit to file.

Be wary of liquidation sales too.

Going out of business sales can be great places to find bargains on necessary items. Be cautious though—you might also get stuck with something that is broken or needs repairs, and if the company has gone out business you have no recourse. When Circuit City went out of business in the spring of 2009 there were media reports about customers taking sealed boxes home to find broken TVs and then being unable to return them. All sales final, really, really means final if the company is gone.

Seek out natural hot springs.

For a free and relaxing afternoon of soaking, seek out natural hot springs. Visit the Web site www.findhotsprings.com to find one in your state. Many of them are places you can hike to easily. Bring along a picnic lunch.

Give up smoking.

A costly habit, not only for the cigarettes themselves, but also for the increased health expenses that smokers incur. It is hard to quit, but this could be the time to do it.

Chances are, you have enough shoes.

Shoe shopping was elevated to a religion in the past decade, and it is time for women to stop worshipping there. You have enough shoes; we know you do. You know you do too.

Bring along the doggie bag.

Restaurant meals are huge. So turn one into your lunch and your dinner by bringing along a plastic container and boxing up half before you start to eat. You can also ask the waiter to bring a doggie bag right after your meal is brought to the table. Don't be shy; this is your food and you can do what you want with it.

Use insider bidding techniques for travel sites.

If you plan to buy a hotel or airline ticket using an auction site like Priceline, check out the site www.biddingfortravel .com first. It is filled with info on how much other people paid and what hotel they actually ended up with.

Review your cell phone bill.

Even if you have an engineering degree and an MBA, you probably can't read your cell phone bill. Most people can't. It seems they're designed to not give enough information by giving too much information. Anytime minutes, "M2M" minutes, "N&W" minutes. Then there are all those other "usage charges" and finally, fees and taxes. Here's what to do. When you have a spare half hour or so someday, call an agent, and have him or her walk you through your bill. We did that recently and found two $10-per-month charges for something the kids had unknowingly subscribed to. We didn't know what it was. The agent explained it, cancelled it, and blocked such items from appearing again.

Satellite and cable contract expired? Be a free agent.

You signed up for that good TV deal a while back, and now you resign yourself to paying that bill every month. If you have a contract, you can't do a whole lot, but most providers allow you to downgrade your service for a small fee should you decide you just plain can't watch 500 channels. The real savings opportunity comes when the contract runs its course. Like a big-name ballplayer, you're a free agent, you can go where you want, and you may be worth a lot. At least the providers will treat you that way. Many have special promotions offering a bonus if you resign your agreement— sometimes it's three months free, sometimes a great bargain on HD service, or maybe a new package. It's worth a session with an agent to figure out your options.

Drop unnecessary land-line charges.

Back in the day, those new services really sounded cool—call waiting, call forwarding, caller ID. But do you really need them? Especially in today's mobile-dominated world? It's a good time to get back to basics with your phone service. Heck, you might even think about getting rid of your land line altogether.

Review your credit card statements.

Probably one of the things you look forward to least every month is receiving—and opening—your credit card bills. Perhaps you're afraid to look at the detail, or perhaps you just open the envelope far enough to see the balance, then shove it in a drawer. If that's the case, you may be missing out on important savings. It's a good idea to at least skim through the detail. One time we had a $5,000 money order from Iowa from someone who had picked up our number while traveling through. Okay, the credit card company caught that one, but what about smaller stuff? ID theft happens, but what happens more often is that we sign up for things that bill automatically, then forget about them—like the $5 a month for our son's Runescape subscription. And if you have your bills paid automatically from your account, that's no excuse— you should still look at the detail.

Ask for a lower credit card interest rate.

Now that sounds brash, doesn't it? Little old you against some cigar-smoking banker asking for a lower rate? Or against a telephone agent who could care less? Surprisingly, you just might get somewhere with this, especially if you've been a good customer over the years. Credit card companies want to keep you. Some may offer the lower rate but with higher fees or a shorter grace period or some other value proposition. But, as always, the way to get the lowest rate of all—zero—is to pay off your balance monthly.

Get rid of storage costs.

By nature, people are pack rats. They like to acquire stuff, but they don't so much like to get rid of it. The problem is, stuff accumulates. Most of us have come a long way from the day when we carried all our belongings off to college in a Gremlin. Many of us have so much stuff we pay to have it stored in one of those expensive storage units, which can cost almost as much per square foot to rent as a nice apartment, incidentally. So if you have too much stuff, be creative. Have a garage sale, give it away, or make a deal to store it at the in-laws'.

Use cash-back credit cards.

Known as "reward cards," these cards pay back a percentage of what you buy each year as cash (or to pay towards your balance). Some, like Discover, pay 1 percent if you reach a certain threshold; some pay even higher percentages for certain items or for shopping in certain stores. For the most part, it's free money, and you can get $100, $200, or more in credit every year, tax free, essentially for doing nothing. Check out the rewards card page at www.creditcard.com/reward.php.

Turn off the lights!

It sounds simple, yet so many of us simply walk out of a room and leave the lights on. Now, sometimes we're leaving a single 23-watt fluorescent bulb on—not a big deal. But if it's a bank of ten 50-watt track lights, that's a big deal. And if its an entire houseful of lights, that's a big deal. Get in the habit of turning off lights as you leave a room. And get those kids to do it, too. You'll not only save electricity, but a lot of bulbs during the year, too.

Replace furnace filters.

Outa sight, outa mind, right? How often do you look at those filters? Well, especially if you live in a dusty environment, you could plant corn on the average filter in a month or two of service. And that restricts the airflow into—and out of— your heating and air conditioning system. That draws more power to move air less effectively. So replace the filters—or get the kind you can wash out. You'll save, and you may feel better, too, as more dust and allergens will be pulled out of the air.

Close drapes at night.

You don't want anyone peeking in your windows, right? But that's not all—your drapes provide an insulation layer preventing cold or warmth from being transmitted through your windows. They block drafts too. Get in the habit of closing drapes and blinds as a last move before going to bed. And if you don't need them open—say, in a spare bedroom—leave them closed.

Know when to use airline miles.

Free tickets are always a good thing. But how free is free? If you use airline mileage, tickets are mostly free indeed (although many airlines are adding booking fees, change fees, and taxes to the "paid for" column). But if you use 25,000 miles to buy a $99 round-trip ticket from San Francisco to Los Angeles, is that a good deal? No. Save those miles for the more expensive flights you might want to take—like San Francisco to Des Moines to visit Aunt Maude, which might set you back $500. Also, miles are good for buying that emergency ticket at the last minute, when prices are always higher. So unless you have millions in your mileage bank, learn to spend wisely, and put that $99 round-trip ticket on your credit card.

Make your own art.

Decorate your blank walls with your own creativity rather than what the poster store has to offer. Painting and drawing are inexpensive ways to craft and give you a tangible reward at the end. Your children's art can also be showcased. In some cities you can make art as a family at your local museum. Check your museum's Web site to see if it has any free hands-on art activity days coming up.

Take the train.

The romance of rail travel, as well as the "see America the way it really is" lure of trains is and always will be with us. But can you save money? If you're smart about it, yes. Amtrak has never been a bargain—it is such an expensive system to run that even with high ticket prices, it loses over $1 billion a year. Typically, if you plan ahead and are flying in competitive markets, flying is cheaper, especially when time is taken into account. But the train can be cheaper if you're going to outlying places, like Glenwood Springs, Colorado, or Charlottesville, Virginia. And if you have to get somewhere "last minute," like inside the fourteen-day advance purchase requirement for air, trains won't cost more. Amtrak sometimes runs specials in which kids ride free with the purchase of an adult ticket. Also, check to see if rail passes are available. All aboard! www.amtrak.com.

Visit college towns for affordable culture.

If you don't want to give up your enjoyment of ballet and music performances but can't afford the high-priced tickets, check in to college programs and performances. Large university towns are always jammed with well-priced cultural offerings, both student performances as well as those given by traveling professionals. Many universities maintain their own orchestras and jazz bands in the music department, and college theatre is always satisfying.

Check out the shopping cart economist.

Read the blog at www.shoppingcarteconomist.com to learn more about what drives food prices up and how you can take steps in your own life to cope with the prices.

Join a CSA—get a vegetable box.

The CSA movement—community sustained agriculture—has spread all over the country. By joining a CSA you will be buying produce directly from the small farmer that produces it, bypassing the middlemen and the grocery store. Once a week a mixed box of whatever was ripe and ready to be picked that week will be available for a fixed price. Usually there is a central pickup spot where members receive their boxes. Produce boxes are not less expensive than buying in the grocery store, but if the wide variety and flavors of fresh-from-the-field produce help you build meals that are less meat-focused, it will pay off. You can also split the cost of a box with another family. Find a CSA program near you by looking at the Local Harvest Web site, www.localharvest .org.

Stuff baked potatoes.

An inexpensive and filling way to feed a family is with stuffed baked potatoes. Bake them, scoop out the insides, and mash with a bit of milk, butter, and sour cream, then add in chopped and spiced meat or cheese or vegetables.

Hold a family meeting.

It is important to bring everyone in the family along with the new money-saving program you'd like to follow. Schedule regular family meetings where everyone gets a chance to air what is on their mind—whether it is to complain about eating baked potatoes for dinner, or to brag about not having spent any money on take-out this week. Discuss how much of a difference everyone can make to the family bottom line, and make sure that the ultimate goal is clear to everyone.

"There are two types of people, my dear. Those who have money, and those who spend money."

—Mary Alice Basye

"Never invest your money in anything that eats or needs repairing."

—Billy Rose

Be creative in the kitchen.

If you have fallen into a rut with the standard things you cook or bake every week, try something new. Get creative about using less-expensive ingredients. Try new recipes and different combinations of old standbys. Those new dishes might end up on the list of family favorites.

Look for energy tax credits.

The laws change every year, but in general, if you make qualifying energy-saving improvements to your home, you'll not only reduce energy costs, but will also become eligible for a host of tax credits. They won't pay for all of your improvements, but will certainly help. Check out the Federal EnergyStar Web site to learn more about Federal credits (www.energystar .gov/index.cfm?c=products.pr_tax_credits) and the North Carolina Solar Center's "DSIRE" database (Database of State Incentives for Renewables & Efficiency) for a more comprehensive summary of federal, state, and local incentives; you can find it at www.dsireusa.org/.

Go generic.

Devoted to a major brand item that you aren't willing to give up for the generic store item? It's time to take the plunge, save the money, and buy the less expensive item. And don't be surprised if it turns out to be the exact same thing. Many large food and consumer product manufacturers produce the generic brand items that sit on the shelf next to their own.

Learn to knit.

Knitting can be a relaxing habit. It can also be a way to make gifts for your friends, clothes for yourself and your family, and even pet sweaters. Plus these items will cost less than they do in a store. Look for less expensive yarns on sale and at online retailers like www.bargainyarns.com. Another money-saving bonus to knitting is that your hands are occupied, so you won't be able to eat expensive snacks.

Take better care of your clothes.

Time to take care of what you have, so that it lasts longer and you won't have to replace it. We don't mean just big things like your car; we mean your clothes too. The longer you can make your basic outfits last, the better for your budget. Hang them up immediately, avoid using bleach (it weakens the fabric) and take care of stains the minute they happen.

Old bread? Make bread pudding!

Jennifer thinks that bread pudding is the bomb when it comes to sweet desserts. So when she has old bread, she makes bread pudding. When life gives you old bread, make bread pudding. You can find a simple recipe at www.momswhothink.com.

Pay half price for event tickets.

For cheap prices on tickets, check out Goldstar. Sherry Crum swears by it—www.goldstar.com. "Buying tickets on Goldstar is great, I've paid half price to see comedians, one of the Cirque de Soleil performances, Chinese acrobats, and more."

What you already have might be enough.

Look around you. Your life is full. So whatever you think you need, whatever you are looking to save money on, chances are it is something you have enough of already. See, even more money saved!

Live the old money life.

Think that rich people own a lot of fancy stuff and spend a lot of money? Guess again. Really wealthy people are sometimes incredibly frugal. They are also incredibly sure of themselves and are not in the least bit concerned about what other people think of them. None of this buying a fancy car so that others will know they are successful. No, they know they are successful, and that is all that matters to them.

So go ahead, act like the very rich. Stop worrying about what other people think. Wear an old tweed jacket that your dad bought twenty years ago, stay with friends when you vacation, and drive your car until it just won't go any further.

Make your lingerie last longer.

Lacy underwear and bras will last far longer and hold their shape longer if you hand wash them. If you don't have the time to hand wash, at least keep them out of the dryer. High heat is the enemy of most fabric, and you can increase the life of your delicate undies if they air dry.

Look for real estate auction bargains.

In the wake of the mortgage and credit crisis, there are homes of all sizes and shapes—well—looking for homes, that is, homeowners. Fire sales are occurring everywhere, and some of the best deals can be found—if you know what you're doing—at auctions. These auctions sell off mostly bank-owned properties coming out of foreclosure, and who is more eager than a bank to get a piece of real estate off their books these days? Right now there are auction companies galore, and even the U.S. government is in on the act. Enter "real estate auction" in your search engine, and maybe your local area, and you'll find them. The Real Estate Disposition Corporation is one of the major players; it holds auctions around the country. Find it at www.ushomeauction .com.

Just make sure to study up ahead on the rules and do's-and-don'ts—the better sites give effective step-by-step instructions and FAQ's on what to do. And be prepared to bring lots of money and/or preapproved credit—you can't buy a house with a credit card.

Make your own glass cleaner.

Skip the blue stuff from the store and instead make your own simple glass cleaner. Reuse a spray bottle (clean it first) and mix together 1 cup of water, 1 cup of rubbing alcohol, and 2 tablespoons of white vinegar.

Share a vacation rental with friends.

Bring down the cost of a vacation rental by sharing it with another family or couple. Two couples sharing a $500 weekend house in the mountains is a far more affordable arrangement than one couple buying themselves that $500 weekend. Yes, it will be a cozier arrangement, but haul out the board games and share the work in the kitchen, and it will be a weekend to remember.

Start a small side business.

Practically every living, breathing person in modern America has the urge to become an entrepreneur. Be your own boss; create your own success; be in charge. Starting a business on the side can save you a lot of dough and give you an outlet for your life's professional energy doing something you really like. It might even someday allow you to walk away from that nine-to-five job.

So how does starting a business save money? Well, especially if it's a home-based business, you can write off a lot of expenses. Writing books or magazine articles? Write off the cost of newspapers, books bought for research, Internet service—and if you follow the rules, you can write off a fraction of the cost of your house and total house expenses. Making stained glass windows for sale? Again, the cost of materials, reference sources, and the space in your house can be deducted. The only catch is—you may have to show the IRS an intent to make a profit (so be as professional about it as possible), and be prepared to make a profit—even a dollar or two, once in a while. It must be a business, not a hobby, and the IRS says that if a business makes a profit in three of five years, it's a real business, no questions asked.

Shop bulk with friends.

It's common knowledge that buying large quantities of anything saves money. But, unless you own a restaurant, just
what would do you do with twenty pounds of Basmati rice
or fifty pounds of dried beans? You'd go crazy trying to find
a place to store it, that's what, and even crazier having to
eat the same thing all the time. Solution: Go shopping with a
friend. Go to the local grocery, or even better, a warehouse
club, and agree to split that two-loaf pack of bread, that
enormous block of cheese, that five-pound bag of M&Ms, or
twelve-pack of chicken noodle soup. It's a fun social thing to
do, too. And splitting the catch can make a fun rainy Saturday
afternoon thing to do too. About that Basmati? The twenty-
pound bag costs $23; two ten-pound bags (still a lot) would
have cost $34. Do the math.

Use salt everywhere.

Salt doesn't just add flavor to food; it is an amazing versatile
mineral that can be used for a variety of budget purposes.
You can remove stains with salt, open clogged drains by adding one-half cup of salt to one quart of hot water and pouring it down the drain, use it as a weed killer, clean brass
and copper with a salt and vinegar paste, and keep ants out
of your cupboard shelves by sprinkling a bit there too. Use
cheap salt instead of high-priced cleaning products.

Use hotel clubs and newsletters.

Like restaurants and their online discounts, joining hotel clubs like Fairmont's President's Club will give you access to special discounts and offers. It costs nothing to join at www .fairmont.com. Your free membership also lets you check in at the President's club counter, and you get free wireless and a newspaper.

Subscribe to budget magazines.

In the past year, several budget-oriented magazines have closed, but several good ones are still standing. Subscribe, share a subscription with a friend, or see if your local library carries copies of:
Woman's Day
Shop Smart
Family Circle
Real Simple

"You cannot keep out of trouble by spending more than you earn."

—Abraham Lincoln

Buy bargain kids' stuff.

To save money on strollers, diaper bags, maternity clothes, pregnancy books, baby clothes, and anything you might need when pregnant or caring for young children, check out www .handmedowns.com. It is a bargain site for moms, with classified ad listings from other moms all over the country.

Buy wine by the case.

Sometimes in order to save money, you have to buy more. Many retail grocery stores and wine shops give case discounts of up to 10 percent if you buy a case of twelve bottles. Sometimes it has to be a case of one kind of wine; other times you can get a discount even if you buy a "mixed" case of different types of wines, as long as you are buying a total of twelve bottles.

Make your own tinted moisturizer.

If you use moisturizer, and you have foundation, you can mix the two together to make a third product—a tinted moisturizer. No need to spend more money to buy that, just put a drop of your foundation into a drop of moisturizer and mix with your finger before applying to your face.

Bring your own cloth shopping bags.

Bringing your own shopping bags to the store is the planet-conscious thing to do nowadays, but it also has a budget pay-off. We don't mean the 5-cents-a-bag credit some stores give you for every bag you save them. The real savings comes from eliminating impulse buying. If you only brought three cloth shopping bags with you, then you will have to stick to your shopping list and can't let yourself pick up a little extra of this and a little extra of that.

Unclutter. Breathe easier.

Take the time to unclutter your living space. Sell or give away what you don't need, and then vow not to clutter your space up again. Once you live in a simpler environment, you won't want to buy frivolous things that might bring the mess back

If you feel overwhelmed by the clutter in your life, check out the amazing Fly Lady system on www.flylady.net. No cost, just a simple thirty-one-day plan to get things clean and neat at home. Day one is simple—shine your sink.

Decorate with blooming plants.

Instead of treating yourself to cut flowers on your dinner table (unless you can cut them for free in your own garden) buy a flowering indoor plant. It is less expensive to buy one pretty plant than a series of bouquets.

Give herbs as gifts.

A simple, no-cost hostess gift is a bouquet of freshly cut herbs from your garden, tied with a simple ribbon. If you don't have a garden, a $1.99 bunch of basil makes an inexpensive gift that any cook will appreciate.

Sunscreen is cheaper than wrinkle cream.

Wrinkle creams are extremely expensive; some run into many hundreds of dollars. Sunscreen, on the other hand, costs less than $10 a tube. Since exposure to the sun causes wrinkles, invest in sunscreen now and use it liberally in order to contain future wrinkle-cream costs.

Get "prompt pay" discounts.

In any situation where you are about to pay cash on the spot for services rather than settle a bill later, ask if there is a "prompt pay" discount. Medical offices, automotive repair places, and other businesses just might knock your bill down a bit if you are paying cash.

Get money back.

There are shopping portals that give you a percentage of your purchase prices back, or help save money off the top. Check out www.extrabux.com and save at stores like Nordstrom, Barnes and Noble, Home Depot, and more. This site puts part of your purchase money back into a PayPal account, or sends you a check.

Go climb a stadium.

Another way to forgo the costly gym membership and still stay in shape is to seek out the local high school stadium and track-and-field area. Run on the track, and then use the stadium stairs for an even tougher workout. Or if there is no stadium nearby, find a tall building—or even a short one with stairwells—and climb the steps. Friends of ours routinely stairstep their way to their 11th floor flat from the parking garage just to get a bit of exercise.

Become a "Maker."

Make magazine sponsors "Maker faires" in San Mateo, California; Austin, Texas; and in Newcastle, UK. Devoted to the extreme D.I.Y. (do it yourself) mentality, these popular faires draw huge crowds who view wacky science projects, hands-on craft and art projects, and just generally celebrate the idea that we should all be the creative "makers" of our own things. Attend and be inspired to take things into your own hands more often. www.makerfaire.com.

Write it all down.

Keep track of absolutely every penny you spend, from the time you get up in the morning until you turn out the lights at night. Write down your coffee purchases, the soda at the gas station, the groceries, and the magazine you bought on the way home. Just write it down, without passing judgment or feeling guilty, but be aware of what you spend. Even just a few days of writing everything down will help you reset your spending habits and become more aware of how it all adds up.

Buy bargain designer furniture.

Model homes in subdivisions are beautifully decorated to make buyers want to live there. But what happens to all of that nice furniture when the homes are all sold and the sales office closes? It too is sold, of course, and at a great discount. Not only is it top-quality furniture, but since no one has ever actually sat on the chairs or eaten at the table, it is unused as well.

Look for a store in your area that sells furniture from model homes. Ask at the sales offices of nearby subdivisions; they might know where the furniture ends up. Jennifer bought two beautiful wood armchairs for $5 apiece last year.

Rip out your lawn.

Is it time to forgo the expense and hassle of maintaining a large front or back lawn and instead go for a more natural look? Check into your neighborhood rules and community laws; some places actually fine residents for not having lush and expensive green lawns. You could replace your high-cost, high-needs lawn with a vegetable garden—so you can lower your food bill at the same time as your lawn bill—or use a natural landscape look with rocks and trees.

Don't be impulsive.

Impulse trips to the grocery store to pick up a little something you forgot the last time almost always lead to you buying more than that one little item you forgot—and the money just adds up from there. We know this scenario sounds familiar—you forgot a jar of peanut butter, but when you go back to the store you also pick up a bag of bagels, some glass cleaner, and a box of Girl Scout cookies from the troop selling in front of the store.

So if you forgot something at the store, learn to live without it until your next planned trip. Your wallet will thank you.

Make only one meal.

You've carefully planned a budget meal for the family, everyone sits down, then the kids take one look at it and say "Bleech." Back to the kitchen drawing board for a different choice for the picky eaters? Not. Make a firm and fast rule—you make one dinner and one dinner only. No quick pot of mac n' cheese, no PB&J sandwiches. Everyone eats the same thing.

Close vents in unused rooms.

If there are rooms in your house that are not regularly used, go ahead and close the vents there. No sense paying to heat or cool a room no one is using. Jennifer closed the vent in the laundry room; the dryer keeps it plenty warm.

Organize your closet!

You have nothing to wear! We know the feeling. But before you rush out to buy something new, why not take the time to sift through everything you have and re-organize? Chances are you will discover things you already own that you haven't worn recently. Put them on and get the quick thrill of a new outfit without the trip to the mall.

"If you want to feel rich, just count the things you have that money can't buy."

—Proverb

Fill your prescriptions over the border.

For whatever reason—and we don't want to get too political here—U.S. drugmakers charge a lot more in the U.S. for pharmaceuticals, especially those with patents that cannot be distributed as generics. If you buy these drugs overseas though, for example, in Canada or Mexico, you can save up to 70 percent occasionally and 30 to 50 percent frequently for common drugs like Celebrex, Nexium or Lipitor. Now, the drug companies say buying drugs this way prevents them from recovering the research and development costs for those drugs, but hey, your money's hard to come by, so go for it. Check out www.drugsfromcanada.com or www.universal drugstore.com. There are others too. You'll have to fax your prescription and take care of a few other details, but it's perfectly legal.

Shop at rummage sales.

A great source of inexpensive—but pedigreed—items is a rummage sale connected to an arts organization. Who knows what supporters might have donated? You might find someone's grandma's old Persian carpet, or Uncle Henry's ancient Mercedes. Jennifer makes it a point to attend the rummage sale sponsored by the symphony in Carmel, California, where she finds lots of great deals on china and silver and other posh items. Church rummage sales and private-school rummage sales can also yield high-end goodies.

Form a children's clothes and toys swap.

Mothers of young children should reach out to each other and organize toy and clothing swaps. The minute you no longer need your stroller it should go to someone who is expecting (with the understanding that it goes back to you should you need it again!). The infant clothes from your neighbor will help you avoid having to buy them all new, and Johnny's old Big Wheel can be passed on to a new arrival on your street. Take the initiative to create the group, and all of the other parents will appreciate your efforts.

Teach your children to make snacks.

Instead of allowing your kids to load up on after-school cookies and crackers, teach them to make simple and less expensive snacks out of tortillas and cheese, fresh veggies, and slices of fruit. Their new snacks will be healthier for their bodies and healthier for your food budget.

Camp in your own backyard.

Our son Julian suggested this idea as a free-but-fun way to entertain kids. Put up the tent, hand them a flashlight, and go back into the house.

Plan free field trips.

Is there a commercial bakery in your town? A large factory of some sort? A historic site by the side of the road? Investigate all of the possible free field trips you can take your children on. Ask someone who has lived in your community for a long time, or ask a school teacher for ideas.

Build a bonfire.

If you live somewhere you can safely and legally build a fire, go for it. You can burn garden leaves and refuse and save yourself an expensive trip to the dump. You can turn it into a fun family afternoon and evening around the fire, roasting marshmallows and telling spooky stories. It will be cheaper than a night at the movies, and your children will remember it longer. One family we know used a backyard bonfire as the centerpiece for a boy's tenth birthday, cooking foil packets of meat and making S'mores, and saving the expense of taking them all to an arcade.

"Money often costs too much."

—Ralph Waldo Emerson

Learn to style your hair with a blow dryer.

The *New York Times* reports that many women are asking their hairdressers to teach them how to style their own hair with a blow dryer as a way to save money. Salons have noticed a drop-off in blowout business. Ask if your own hairstylist is willing to teach you a few professional tricks with a blow dryer and a round brush.

Recycle your electronics.

Before you buy a new electronic gadget, try to get some money from your old one that you can use towards your new purchase. There are technology recycling Web sites that will pay you— not much, but something—for things like old iPods. Check out www.myboneyard.com and www.gazelle .com.

Can your own fruits and vegetables.

Master food preserver Karen Brees advises "You'll save the most money by growing your own vegetables and fruits and canning or freezing the harvest. You'll save slightly less if you patronize 'pick your own' orchards or berry patches and farmers' markets. You'll still save if you buy foods in season at bulk foods warehouses or your local grocery store, when they're cheaper and more plentiful." So get out there and can!

Teachers save money.

Teachers are getting creative about ways to save in the class-room. California teacher Mel Aubert told us "We are now running one-sided copies on the back sides of other used papers. So if I need to run a one-sided script, I will run it on the back of maybe someone's leftover one-sided math test. We are also using white boards rather than paper to do warm up work." The same idea would work well in any office environment.

Make your own pet food.

Yes, you really can make your own pet food. In the long run it will be less expensive, and healthier for your pet. Check out the info on www.make-stuff.com/cooking/petfood.html. Your pets will love you even more than they already do.

Make your own baby stuff.

The cool folks at Make-Your-Own-Baby-Stuff (www.make-your-own-baby-stuff.com) have all kinds of information about how to stay out of the pricey baby stores and instead make your own baby clothes, accessories, bedding, nursery décor, and even homemade baby food. Even if you don't have a baby, the site has great ideas for things you can make for baby showers and baby gifts.

Learn to sew.

Do you have a sewing machine in a closet somewhere? Time to pull it out. If you never knew or don't remember how to use the thing, ask your mother or your grandmother or the older woman next door. One of them may know how and offer to teach you.

Once you've dusted off your sewing skills, get to work making simple things for your house—pillows and couch slip-covers—those are the biggest money-savers nowadays. You can make simple women's clothing, but understand that your children really, really won't want you making anything for them.

Check out free business marketing ideas.

Small businesses and independent professionals can now skip the cost of an expensive Web site and go straight to the free online social marketing world of Facebook. Jennifer markets two small businesses that way with great results at absolutely no cost. You might also use a free blog to replace a Web site, or use the services of Constant Contact (www .constantcontact.com) to stay in touch with your customers and clients instead of costly mailings.

Get free business cards.

Out of your fancy business cards? Instead of reprinting those, why not switch to the free business cards you can get from Vista Print at www.vistaprint.com? Vista Print will send you 250 business cards for just the price of shipping if you keep their advertisement on the back of your card. Pay an extra $5.99 to remove the Vista advertising and it is still among the cheapest ways to get business cards. Here's another way: with today's modern printers and pre-packaged business card forms, you can also print your own.

Coffee smoothies at home.

At our house we hardly ever finish the entire pot of coffee. Sound like your house too? So instead of tossing it out pour it into ice trays and freeze the coffee in individual cubes. You can use the frozen cubes to make your own frozen coffee drinks at home and avoid the several dollars at the café.

Combine your errands.

Cut back on using extra gas (and remember to poll your neighbors to see if they want to ride along) when running errands. Draw up a list of several things you need to do and make one long extended trip, rather than several short ones. Remember, it is the little short trips for something small that can end up costing you if you pick up an impulse item.

Check out HULU.

Can you skip cable all together and just hulu instead? Check out www.hulu.com for the many shows and movies you can watch on your computer for free. You won't have to give up *Family Guy, The Daily Show*, or *Saturday Night Live*.

Look for inexpensive team sports clubs.

Check out the YMCA, your local community college, or a local church to se what low-cost team sports opportunities they might offer. A little pickup soccer, basketball, or even Ultimate Frisbee can cut the fat—and save a lot, too.

Travel where the dollar is strong.

As we write this in the spring of 2009, the dollar is strong and has great buying power in Mexico, Canada, and Australia, as well as most of Latin America and much of Southeast Asia. Always look for destinations where your dollars go farther against the local currency. This hasn't been the case for Americans in a while, so if you have the time and the money to travel, take advantage of it while it lasts!

Use recycled printer cartridges.

Before you head to the office supply store for another ink cartridge for your home or office printer, check to see if you can find a recycled cartridge for less. Re-inks at www.re-inks .com has a large selection.

Be aware that the print quality might not be as good, but recycled printer cartridges may serve well for your everyday needs. You can always use the name-brand printer cartridges for important projects where image really counts.

Get free.

Check out the selections at www.download.com for free software. Lots of choices for developer tools, graphic design software, security software, and software for iTunes and iPods.

Rent a wreck!

Look first at the prices and cars available from Rent-a Wreck before you rent a brand new vehicle. With offices in forty-eight states, RentAWreck (www.rentawreck.com) maintains a fleet of safe and reliable used vehicles that will cost far less than cars from those other guys.

Hire your children.

If you have a small home-based business, don't forget that you can hire your own children to do tasks for you. Ask them to clean the office, organize files, or back up your computer (all children know more about your computer than you do). You can pay them a reasonable sum, and deduct it from your taxes.

Get married on a budget.

Weddings are among the costliest events in anyone's life, but there are many ways to bring the costs down. Check out the wikihow.com/save-money-on-your-wedding-ceremony-and-reception for a long list of ideas. For example, have your wedding and reception in the same place to cut down on transportation costs. Cancel that limo!

Skip the fancy cake.

Cakes for all occasions are expensive when you order them from a custom bakery, so serve chic cupcakes instead. You can cut costs on wedding cakes and cakes for other special events by having a cupcake tier—a three-stage display of cupcakes. Everyone loves cupcakes, and they won't notice the cake is missing. You can easily make a cupcake tier yourself. It's far easier than making your own wedding cake.

Know when to get married.

Many wedding venues charge less for events held on Fridays or on Sundays. Saturday is the primo day for weddings, so choose another day if you want to try to get a better deal.

Save a slice.

A loaf of bread lasts twice as long (and your waist is thinner) if you make an open-faced sandwich. Grilled cheese and tomatoes, avocado and cheese—pile it up high (so maybe your waist won't be so thin after all) on one piece only.

Choose unprocessed.

When grocery shopping, remember that the less done to the food, the cheaper it is. Plus the closer to its natural state, the better it is for your body and your budget. Think about this—a bag of beans costs 89 cents; a can of cooked beans costs 99 cents. Seems like just difference of 10 cents, right? Not. The bag of beans will make seven cups of beans; the can has only one cup of beans. The difference is not a dime; the can is five times as costly as the raw bag of beans.

Keep tabs on your credit card balances.

We've always found it kind of amusing that people can tell you to the nearest penny how much a gallon of gas costs, but couldn't tell you within $300 what their current month's charges are on their credit cards. Plastic fantastic, charge away, and don't worry about it until the bill comes at the end of the month. Oops! Can't afford to pay that. Now it's a balance, with interest, and repeat the cycle. Our view is that you can keep your expenses under control by doing something very simple—keep track of your credit card balances and activity through the month. Some of you numbers-geeky folks can keep track in your head; for the rest of us, it means a once-in-a-while check of your credit card activity online. It's easy. Or it should be, anyway—if it isn't, get a different credit card.

"If you think nobody cares if you're alive, try missing a couple of car payments."

–Earl Wilson

Live on a budget.

Ooooh, yuck—the "b" word: budget. Endless hours of planning and reconciliation each month to come up with how many lattes each of you is allowed to buy—two a week, no more, and better not add a "classic coffee cake" to the order. Nope. Doesn't work. But did you know you don't really have to go through this line-by-line grind? Living on a budget the smart way says that you create allowances for family members (sort of like when you were a kid, right?). Everyone can spend as they please—up to the limit. Total freedom—within the limit. And a limit for the family, too, not just each individual, so things like movie night and the weekend away come from the family allowance. For more on a "living on a budget" plan that really works, see our *Pocket Idiot's Guide to Living on a Budget*.

Reward family members for living on a budget.

As physiologist and psychologist Ivan Pavlov demonstrated years ago, people are naturally motivated by rewards. So how does that connect with the idea of saving money? Simply this: if family members—or you, for that matter—haven't quite gotten in the habit of saving money or living on a budget, try a small reward. "If we cut our expenses by $200 this month, guess what—we all get to go out for pizza and a movie!" Or, if we cut $200 a month for the entire year, maybe there's a nice weekend away, or an upgraded hotel on our next trip. Whatever. You get the idea. A reward system for doing the right thing with your money encourages the right behaviors. Just don't make the reward bigger than the amount saved, of course.

Do your own taxes.

Well, this one isn't for everyone; if you own a corporation or three rental properties, the task can be daunting. But for a lot of folks, a simple day or two filling out forms will get it done, and it really isn't that bad if you can run a calculator and read directions. And the IRS Web site (www.irs.gov) is a pretty good place to get those trickier questions answered. You'll save on tax prep fees—maybe $150 or so, maybe more—and here's what we like—you'll get a better handle on your own finances.

Fire your mutual funds.

For years, traditional "open-ended" mutual funds were the way to go with most of your investment stash. Leave the driving to someone else; they manage your funds and give the diversification you need; you're free to go on about your life and sleep at night. But like any other service, there's a price, and for mutual funds it's fees. When all are taken together—the management fees and especially the sinister "12-b-1" marketing fees—where your money is spent to attract more investors—you can lose an average of 1.3 to1.5 percent of your investment value each year. Over time, that's a lot. There's an alternative—exchange traded funds, or ETFs—which track indexes or baskets of stocks and add fees something closer to 0.5 percent. That one percent can make a big difference, and by the way, your tax outcome is usually better too, for with ETFs you typically only pay capital gains when you sell.

Clean and refresh your deck.

Have a wooden deck behind your house? All that sun, rain, snow, and dirt over time will make your beautiful wood fade into a dull shade of grey—or worse. Decks are hard to maintain, and many people give up on them after ten or fifteen years and replace them—an expensive proposition. But you really can renew your deck; it isn't too hard. Rent a pressure washer. You might also get a deck scrub; oxalic-acid-based varieties work best. Scrub with the wash if it's really bad, then "hit the deck" with a widely fanned pressure wash, and watch your deck really come clean. Finally, apply a high-quality stain with some kind of hardener, such as Duck-back Products' "SuperDeck"—you'll once again have beautiful wood and a sense of accomplishment.

"There are two times in a man's life when he should not speculate: when he can't afford it, and when he can."

—Mark Twain

Bring a calculator to the store.

Nowadays, more than ever, it's important to get the biggest bang for your hard-earned bucks. Easy to say, but sometimes it's hard to do. Manufacturers seem to deliberately confuse you with odd-sized packages—any trip down the detergent or cereal aisle will confirm this. When they offer three pounds, eleven ounces of detergent for $5.95 and four pounds, 15 ounces for $6.69, which is the better deal? Does it make sense to spring for the larger size? It depends. Now, most groceries mark the cents per ounce on the shelf next to the product, and that helps. But you don't see this in everywhere. Now, about those bags of bird seed at the ranch supply store . . . A calculator is real cheap, and it comes in handy—take one with you when you shop. And who cares if you look like a nerd—if you're saving money. Heck if you really are a nerd, you can do the math in your head—so much the better!

Buy ahead when you can.

Twelve double rolls of toilet paper for $6.77; twenty-four double rolls, on sale, for $7.77. Yes, it happens, and to be sure, toilet paper doesn't spoil or go bad. So stock up! Put the extra rolls in some unused under-sink cabinet in one of your bathrooms. It is but one example of smart shopping. Now, don't be so-o-o-o smart that you can't get your car in the garage, but if you buy, say, two boxes of Kleenex a week, maybe that ten-pack offer at the grocery or at the warehouse club makes sense. Make a little room and you'll save a lot of dough.

Make your own dips.

If you love potato chips or nachos with a sour cream dip of some sort—say, French Onion—ooooh, doesn't that sound good right now?—you're looking at $2.50 or more just for the dip. And you had better plan to use that much, pretty quickly, or else it will go bad. So you eat too much, or end up throwing half of it away, right? Well, there's another way— simply keep plain sour cream on hand (it's good for other stuff too, so you'll get more use out of it) and a few packages of dry onion soup, like the Lipton's kind. Just mix a little from a soup packet into your sour cream, and voila! You can try other flavors too, and nothing goes to waste.

Don't drink soda.

Time was when Peter was fairly well addicted to Coke and Dr Pepper and had a cold can somewhere in the house all day long. But as we all know, soda is mainly just sugar water—not particularly good for you—and it's an expensive habit. Besides, drinking so much of what's in those cans leaves you with lots of recycling to do. Sure, soda isn't as expensive as cigarettes or alcohol; we'll give you that. But when other family members climb on board, three or four twelve-packs a week really add up. So Peter quit. Cold turkey. The springboard was the discovery of lime juice, one of the key ingredients in the Coke mixture. It's really good, really refreshing, not as bad for you as soda, and easy to make from concentrate. So, no more Coke cans around the house, and now the stuff is more of a treat when he (and the boys) go to a restaurant.

Cook several meals at once.

Another great way to save time and money and avoid costly trips to the grocery store is to plan your meals for the week, shop for all of your ingredients, and then set aside a weekend afternoon in which to cook them all. Label and freeze for use throughout the week

Put eggs on your menu.

Eggs can be elegant and inexpensive main dishes. A dozen eggs costs less than $2 at most major grocery stores and will feed a high-protein meal to a family of four. Kids are always happy to have breakfast for dinner, so toast that day old bread and give them eggs and toast for dinner.

Check the grocery store receipt.

Double check your grocery store receipts before leaving the store. What are you looking for? Make sure that the sale items you bought were rung up with the discounted price. It can be tricky to find the right brand and size of a sale item. Also make sure that any coupons you used were rung up and properly credited to your total. Another reason to check the receipt is to see what kind of coupons have been printed on it. Purchases frequently prompt coupons for rival products, and it is worth looking to see if you can use that coupon to save money on your next visit.

Sweeten your budget with honey.

Honeybees are an important part of the natural cycle. If you have a love for honey and an interest in insects, consider keeping a bee box in your own backyard. If you have a large piece of rural property, you can have several bee boxes and rent them out to farmers during the pollination season. With just one box, you will have enough free honey to satisfy your sweet tooth and that of many of your friends. A great place to learn basic information is at www.gobeekeeping.com.

Try used sports equipment.

Before you head out to buy new sports equipment and supplies for yourself or your children, check to see if you can find it used at Play it Again Sports. They buy, sell, and trade new and used name-brand sports equipment—everything from hockey and basketball to wakeboarding and snowboarding gear. There are stores across the country, find one near you at www.playitagainsports.com.

Rent your textbooks.

Textbooks have always been expensive, and that doesn't look likely to change in the future. Students have long sought out sources for used textbooks, but now you can also rent copies of required textbooks. Check out www.chegg.com to see if they have the books you need for your classes.

Skip the plastic bags.

Why buy plastic sandwich bags when the world gives them to you for free? Reuse any and all plastic produce bags and shopping bags for storage instead of buying boxes of plastic bags. Wash and reuse heavy zipper-type plastic bags too. You can also use plastic storage containers that you already have instead of buying more plastic bags. Once you get out of the habit of buying new, and into the habit of reusing what you have, you will wonder why you ever spent money on plastic.

Save with Entertainment Books.

The Entertainment Book has been a fund-raising stalwart for decades. No doubt you bought one once to support your local school, marching band, or service organization. Time to buy one again, if there is one available for your area. If you purchase online midyear, the books are available at half price. Visit www.entertainment.com. Jennifer bought one for her area, Sacramento, in March 2009, for $22.

These books are packed with coupons to remove and redeem in stores and restaurants. They also give you access to online deals and discounts that you can claim with a print-out coupon or by clicking through sites to make a direct claim for your entertainment discount.

Only buy an Entertainment Book if you are leading the kind of life that includes going out to restaurants, activities, and events. For many years Jennifer and Peter were home with small kids and hardly went out, so it didn't make sense to have a book of coupons they didn't use. If you are a homebody, skip this.

Trade DVDs and CDs with friends.

Instead of buying the latest and greatest music and movies the minute they are available, why not form an informal media swap club with your friends and neighbors. Have everyone bring at least four DVDs or CDs that they are willing to trade, and swap amongst yourselves. Keep track of who got what, as maybe you want to trade for it the next time!

Watch cheaper movies.

A night out at the movies can put a big dent in your budget, but there are several sources for discounts on movie tickets, including through the Entertainment Guide, your membership in Costco, Sam's Club, or AAA. There are also local offers available at grocery stores (ask at the check stand about special offers and coupons), the movie theater itself (ask the manager when the best prices are), or in the newspaper.

Some movie theaters offer free family movies throughout the summer months. Ask your local movie theater if they have a program like that.

Scent your clothing.

Stop buying fancy scented dryer sheets, and instead, make your own scented dryer bags. Cut out two squares of unbleached cotton muslin, 4-by-4 inches. Look in the remnant section of the fabric store for inexpensive scraps. Fill with dried lavender seeds or dried rosemary, and sew up the edges.

Toss the dryer bag in with your clothing and let it add a pleasant scent to your clothes and sheets.

Walk your dog.

Healthy pets have fewer pricey visits to the vet, and the best way to keep your pet healthy is through exercise. You could both use it, so get out there and walk your dog for free. An investment in everyone's well-being and mental health.

"A nickel ain't worth a dime anymore."

—Yogi Berra

Meet your local dollar store.

Once only found in rural communities, dollar stores are now everywhere. The biggest chains are the Dollar Tree (www .dollartree.com), Family Dollar (www.familydollar.com), and 99 Cents Only (www.99only.com). Look for the store locators on their Web sites to find a store nearest you.

What can you buy for a dollar? Almost anything. Cleaning products, brand-name beauty products, toiletries, paper goods, holiday items, canned and boxed food items, even clothing. Where does it come from? Closeouts from other retail stores, returned goods to the manufacturer, or large bulk buys that bring the cost down. Be warned though: While some things are great values (look for the brand-name items you'd see in a grocery store), many items are actually worth less than the dollar the store is charging. So always ask yourself—is this really worth more than a dollar? Am I really saving here, or does it just seem that way?

Air dry your dishes.

A simple way to cut down on energy costs is to stop using the dry cycle on your dishwasher. If you turn your dishwasher on after dinner, early in the evening, you can easily open the door once the washing cycle has ended and let your dishes dry all night with the door open (careful, you don't want anyone tripping on it in the dark, so be sure and warn family members what you are planning to do). Once you hear the wash cycle end, check the dial to see if it has begun the dry cycle, and then just turn the knob to off and open the door.

Move to a cheaper city.

OK, so it's not a decision to be taken lightly, nor one to be done on a yearly basis. But hear this: No matter where you live, there is probably a cheaper place to live. Now, the cheapest places to live may not be the perfect places to live, but that's what cars and air fare bargains are for. As a co-author of *Cities Ranked & Rated—More Than 400 Metropolitan Areas Evaluated in the U.S. and Canada,* Peter can tell you that more than two thirds of the 375 major metropolitan areas in the U.S. have a cost of living index below the U.S. average. Why? Because the other third are so darned expensive that they drag the average up to where it is. Avoid cities like Chicago and New York and try ones like Lexington and Rochester. It's a life decision, yes, and you may decide not to do it, but it's worth looking at alternatives. You may find a copy of the book at your local library or you can find this information online at co-author Bert Sperling's www .bestplaces.net.

"A bank is a place where they lend you an umbrella in fair weather and ask for it back when it rains."

—Robert Frost

Move to a cheaper neighborhood.

Just as you can enjoy San Francisco's amenities from Sacramento or Chicago's amenities from Racine, you can also enjoy these cities or any other from a less expensive neighborhood within the city. Particularly if you like older homes and aren't too dependent on the local school system, there are bargains galore in "inner" neighborhoods—not run-down city cores necessarily, but forgotten-about areas often inside a city's beltway, away from where the McMansion boom is heard loudest. They're close to everything, and have mature trees and landscaping, quiet streets, and well-built homes that don't look like they were furbished by Home Depot. Every city has them. Contact your real estate professional, or visit Sperling's Best Places (www.bestplaces.net) to compare specific zip codes in an area.

Downsize your house.

Stop and think about it. Do you really need 4,600 square feet, complete with a 200-square-foot entry, a 600-square-foot master suite (with a master bath larger than most bedrooms)? Answer: Unless you have a huge family or lots of in-laws living aboard, probably not. Driven in part by the recession, Americans are starting to think about this. Quality and design are winning out over quantity. The Not So Big House movement, spawned by architect Sarah Susanka's book by that name, is getting big. After all, the average new home of some 1,500 square feet in the mid-1970s became some 2,200 square feet by the late 1990s. Yet did we grow that much? No—as a species, we're about the same size, and if 1,500 square feet did it then, it would probably do it now.

Buy a storage shed.

We suggested in another tip that you get rid of that storage unit and its monthly exorbitant per-square-foot cost. How? Sell or donate that stuff you don't really need, or store it at the in-laws, if they have room. Here's another idea: a storage shed in your backyard. For $1,000 or $1,500 or so, you could get one of those prefab jobs. If that saved $60 a month in storage costs, it would pay for itself in a reasonable time and add to the value of your property. You would also take better care of those garden power tools and implements; they would last longer. The only downside—you might collect more junk! So imagine your life with a shed—it just might make sense.

Get a programmable thermostat.

Programmable thermostats are a pretty old idea really. The notion is to be able to set it by time of day to keep the house warmer or cooler according to your preference, when you're actually home, and when you might be in bed under blankets and not need that hothouse indoor climate. Most of these units cost between $40 and $70 and are easy to buy and install. Some utility companies are even offering them for free or at reduced prices—check to see if yours is on this bandwagon.

Don't get caught naked in a swimming pool.

What we mean is—don't buy one if you don't absolutely have to—and we can't think of many situations where one absolutely has to! They're expensive to build. They add to property value, but only at a fraction of what they cost. Then there's all that upkeep—chemicals, pool service, heating, even the water that goes into the darned things. And then there's the fact that in most of the country, it's too darned cold to use them most of the year. If tempted, the best way to deal with that temptation is to 1) find a swim club or athletic club (other benefits too), 2) find a local lake or park allowing swimming for those really hot days, or 3) find a friend, neighbor, or relative who has one. Offer to bring steak dinner and all they can drink twice a week—and you'll still save a ton of money over the cost of owning a pool.

Get rid of the phantom menace.

Lots of electric things around your house—even when they're "off"—use power. Pretty much anything with one of those black transformer "bricks" on the cord uses power in an off state. Want to know how we know? Because they're warm. That means they're converting electricity into heat. And those TVs that come on instantly—you know how they do that? By keeping a certain amount of power flowing through their systems at all times. And your laser printer? A small wire is kept hot just in case you want to print something. Bottom line: There are a lot of electricity "phantoms" around your house. If you aren't using something, especially for long periods of time, unplug it.

Do financial forensics.

No, you won't need a face mask, gloves or a scalpel (we don't think so, anyway). But one of the first steps any individual or family can take to get their expenses under control is to learn more about them. So the "financial forensics" exercise involves just that—sit down with your family and figure out where everything goes. You'll discover a lot just discussing spending patterns at the kitchen table; you'll learn about other spending patterns by simply watching all the expenses for, say, a week. Observe just how many Red Bulls and caramel lattes are coming out of that family budget. Remember, we're just observing here, not blaming anyone for their behavior, so keep it out in the open and light. You'll be amazed what you find out—and if you do decide to build a budget later on, you'll be ready, and you'll be realistic.

"Money can't buy friends, but it can get you a better class of enemy."

—Spike Milligan

If you can count your money, you don't have a billion dollars."

—J. Paul Getty

Learn how supermarkets price.

They call it "merchandising." You might call it "weird." Why is a gallon of milk $4.39—more than a gallon of apple juice or maybe even orange juice? That same milk might be sold for $5.49 for two gallons—but you have to buy two gallons. What's going on here? Simply—and all stores do it—the store is probably trying to subsidize other "loss leaders," that is, bargains, to compete more effectively with other stores. So the milk is expensive—everyone has to buy it, right? In the meantime, they mark down the bags of oranges or the tri-tip. Once you understand this, you can navigate your way to the bargains (the weekly newspaper insert can help) and away from the "cash cows." Such cash cows, like most cereals and bottled or canned beverages, can be bought in bulk at your warehouse club and stored.

Restructure your credit cards.

Businesses restructure their debt every now and then, so why shouldn't you? Businesses will pay off old loans and get new ones, to get better terms, to switch banks, or for a host of other reasons. Why shouldn't you? That United Mileage Plus card you got years ago while traveling a lot on business—just how much good does that do you now? That Sears Master-Card, which just raised its interest rate to 23 percent? That store card that just started charging $10 out of the blue for a phone payment? Things change, and you need to change with them. Moreover, many businesses give their best bennies to new customers, at the expense of old ones who they figure just aren't going to switch. This is probably counter to what you thought, right—that the longest customers are treated best? Not always. It sometimes pays to start fresh with your accounts, especially if your credit is good.

Shop for freebies.

Check out the Shop4Freebies site at www.shop4freebies .com. Jennifer recently got a coupon in the mail for a free frozen dinner after filling out an online form. The selection changes every twenty-four hours, so you can score all kinds of things, from toothpaste and underwear to grocery items and small gifts. Visit often to see what they have.

Visit the back of the grocery store.

Always include a visit to the far back reaches of your grocery store, where you might find a shopping cart full of drastically reduced and discontinued items. The best buys are high-priced gourmet food items that didn't sell and jams and cookies that are delicious indulgences costing far less than the original price. Ask at the checkout if they have a closeout section anywhere in the store.

Don't pay the "Chardonnay" tax.

Dorothy Gaiter and John Brecher, the wine experts at the *Wall Street Journal,* believe that many Chardonnays on restaurant wine lists are "grossly overpriced." Why? Because Chardonnay is popular, and restaurants know that many people will order it, they mark it up a dollar or two. They suggest you skip the Chardonnay then, when you are out for the evening, and instead order a white wine like a Reisling or a Gruner-Veltliner.

Simple pasta is the best.

This inexpensive pasta meal is perfect—plain pasta, olive oil, garlic, and Parmesan cheese. Add a salad or a loaf of bread you've made yourself, and you have a budget gourmet meal.

Try a Zipcar.

Zipcars are ride-share cars now available in a dozen big urban cities and some college campuses. Check www.zipcar .com to find out if Zipcar operates near you. Join and pay a membership fee, and then you can use the cars on an hourly basis as needed. You won't need to own your own car any longer; neither will you have to worry about overnight parking or a garage.

Stretch your dollars.

The dedicated money-saving blog at Dollar Stretcher (www .stretcher.com) has lots of great ideas, daily updates, and articles on all manner of money issues. It's worth signing up for the Dollar Stretcher's e-mail alerts to stay up on the news.

Download music instead of buying CDs.

Compare the price of the newly released CD you just have to have with the cost of buying the best of its tunes from iTunes or at Amazon.com. At as little as 79 cents a download, that's a bargain. It is hard to give up the idea of having the entire "album" worth of music, but by buying a few affordable songs the legal way, you will be able to enjoy the music and know the musicians are being paid for their work. (This is a nice way of saying that, no matter how tight your budget, please don't download illegally or burn a copy of the CD your friend bought.)

"What difference does it make how much you have? What you do not have amounts to much more."

—Seneca

Skip the fancy fruit salad.

Convenience is one thing; hugely overpaying for it is another. Don't try to save a tiny bit of time in the kitchen by buying an already cut-up fruit salad. For about the same amount of money you can buy the fruits individually, cut them up, and package your own individual fruit salads to take to lunch.

Avoid one-time-use items.

Are you about to buy something that can only be used one time and then tossed? Think again. You might decide it isn't worth it, that there is a way to do without it, or that there is a way to reuse the item in a clever and budget-minded way. It's better for the planet, better for your wallet, and you'll be one step closer to being a more mindful consumer. And before you throw something out, whether it is a plastic bag, some aluminum foil, or a ruined pair of panty hose, stop and ask yourself if there is a way it can reasonably be used again.

Sleep free in Paris.

Writers can take advantage of an amazing opportunity to sleep free in Paris at the venerable Left Bank bookstore, Shakespeare & Company. Over the years many writers and aspiring writers have slept on cots amidst the books. The only requirement from the bookstore owner is that they read a book a day. You can contact the bookstore at www .shakespeareandcompany.com.

Appreciate what money can't buy.

Next time you feel constrained by your newly shrunken wallet, focus instead on appreciating all of the things that money can't buy. We know it can't buy happiness, but it also can't buy the well-being of your family, a beautiful sunset or a quiet moment with your loved ones.

One woman recently told the *New York Times* that because she can't afford to shop as much as she used to, she is no longer "seeking happiness from material things." Well put.

Go to a brand new university.

Most U.S. colleges and universities have been around for one hundred years or more. But not all. The demand for college education and the overcrowding in some schools and some states has led to the establishment of new colleges and universities. A good example is the new University of California campus at Merced. Merced was a sleepy little agricultural town before the new university arrived, and it's still in transition. That means it's less expensive than most college towns. But there's more—a new student here can get in on the ground floor of that transition and enjoy the attention of a small college environment while getting a full and highly desirable University of California degree. Look for new university branch campuses, which can be found in up-and-coming college towns or as extensions in your city.

Wear a budget wedding dress.

Before buying an expensive gown for the big day, why not go and see what is for sale on www.preownedweddingdresses.com. You can literally save thousands by buying a designer gown that has been worn just once before. The site offers a large selection of top-designer dresses and a continually changing inventory, so if you don't see what you like this week, you can try again next week.

Keep your teeth healthy.

Don't skimp on visits to the dentist, as keeping your teeth healthy is a low-cost way to make sure the rest of you stays healthy. Oral health is directly related to your general health in that reports link low-grade infection in the mouth (periodontal disease) to systemic illnesses such as cardiovascular disease (heart disease), respiratory ailments (pulmonary or lung disease), and poor pregnancy outcomes (babies born too small and too soon). Persons with diabetes are also at increased risk for periodontal infections. If you can't see your regular dentist, your local community college might have a dental hygienist-training program that offers reduced fees when their students attend to you.

Find cosmetic laser treatment bargains.

Check the Web site of your area's biggest cosmetic surgeons and see if they have any clinical studies open for enrollment that you can participate in for reduced prices or perhaps at no cost. Laser clinic staff need training with new equipment, and if you are willing to participate and help them learn the craft, you might be able to get treatment at no cost.

Take a bath with fragrant herbs.

For a relaxing and low-cost evening, soak in an herb-infused tub. You can make your own bath sachets using dried lavender, rosemary, and other heavily scented herbs. Using an old handkerchief or a 12-inch-square piece of muslin or cheesecloth, simply pile up the dried herbs in the center of the cloth and gather up the edges, tie with string or a stray piece of ribbon. Start your bath water, drop in the sachet, and let it soak in the water to give the room a delicious smell. Slip in and soak to your heart's content. Add some relaxing music and you could be in any expensive spa . . .

Get beautiful in your kitchen.

Much of what we use for dinner can also be used to make simple beauty products—use leftover avocado as a moisturizing face mask, egg white as a tightening face mask, olive oil as a hair treatment, or rub it on your elbows to smooth dried skin. No need for pricey beauty potions. Check your refrigerator first.

Swap flowers.

Do you grow roses, but long to have a vase of hydrangeas on your dining room table? Instead of going to the florist, why not arrange a flower swap among your neighborhood gardeners? Turn it into a social event by choosing a date and time for all of the gardeners to wander freely amongst each other's gardens with their snips, gathering afterwards for coffee and cookies.

Play the grocery game.

Terry Gault founded The Grocery Game in Southern California, but this money-saving opportunity is now available in all fifty states. It is hard and tedious work to stay on top of all of the various sales, specials, and coupons that arrive every week, so instead many people subscribe to the Grocery Game, which does the work for them. Sign up at www.thegrocerygame.com and every week you will get a detailed list of what is available in your area, broken down by store, matched with coupons and specials, and tailored to your needs.

Visit Mary Jane's online farm.

Mary Jane Butters is one smart farm girl. She has built a business around a down-home, do-it-yourself country aesthetic. In books and magazines and, of course, on her farm (she runs a learn-to-farm camp), she spreads the farm-girl philosophy. Spend-time-on-the-farm girl blogs on her Web site, where you can learn useful, budget-minded skills from the contributors. Want to make your own laundry soap? Make a picture frame out of chicken wire? Visit www.maryjanesfarm.org.

Don't eat anything you can buy at a gas station.

Yes, you need to fill your car at a gas station, but you will be better off financially if you don't buy anything to eat there. Not only is it expensive, but, um, most if not all of what is for sale there is not in the least bit healthy. So don't buy it. Your body and your wallet will thank you.

Put worms to work.

Another way to make your own rich fertilizer and potting soil is having worms eat your garbage. Yes, worms. In your house. Eating your garbage. Learn more at www.worm woman.com. It really isn't nearly as creepy as it sounds and is a great way to cut back on waste and give your children a science lesson.

Save movie money with Netflix or Redbox.

Is it time to cut back on the neighborhood video store altogether and sign up for Netflix? Even cheaper than Netflix is the emerging rental vending business, Redbox. Redbox rents first-run films for $1 a day. You get it out of a vending box at the grocery store. To find a Redbox location near you, go to www.redbox.com.

Set your printer to "draft."

Use less toner or ink in your home printer by using the "draft" function. Remember to switch it back to normal when you are printing out important documents!

Handy women.

Ladies, don't be afraid to roll up your sleeves and fix what is busted. If you don't know how to do what needs doing, check out www.bejane.com for all of the do-it-yourself info geared to women. You will "Be Jane" in no time.

Use blogs to get money smart.

You aren't alone in your desire to save money nowadays. Keep up with the attempts of others to make their dollars last longer by reading their stories on money blogs like www.notmadeof money.com, www.moneysavingmom.com, and www.howisave money.com. Join the community of budget-minded folks and you will pick up new ideas as they discover and share them.

Save for college at Upromise.com.

Sign up with Upromise and start building up college savings for yourself or your children through their affiliate program. Anywhere from 1 to 25 percent of the money you spend with their vendors—big sites like JCPenney, Nordstrom, Sears, and even Expedia—goes into your Upromise account to be used in a 529 college savings plan. You can also register your credit cards and get money paid into your account by dining at any one of 8,000 restaurants around the country. It doesn't cost anything to sign up, and while it won't pay for college on its own, it is a great way to slowly build up a small chunk to help pay the overall cost.

Get free phone info.

Those calls to 411 add up, more than $1 a piece sometimes. So instead, if you find yourself in need of a phone number and can't look it up online, just dial 1-800-FREE-411. You will have to listen to a short commercial first (that is why they can do it for free) but it is worth it to save the money and get the number you needed anyway.

Find an outlet mall.

When planning your family vacations, you might as well check to see if you will be in the vicinity of any major outlet malls. You can find a complete listing of outlet malls across the country at www.outletbound.com.

"Money will buy you a pretty good dog, but it won't buy you the wag of his tail."

—Henry Wheeler Shaw

Bowl for cheap.

Sign up at www.brunswick.com to get coupons and money-saving deals from Brunswick, the big bowling company. Visit their site first to see if there is a Brunswick bowling alley near you, and sign up online if there is!

Recycle old blue jeans.

Your old blue jeans can do all kinds of things for you, don't toss them out! Check out the info at www.wisebread.com/twenty-five-things-to-do-with-old-jeans to see what you can turn them in to.

Regift the gifts of Christmas.

You got a really nice set of purple towels for a holiday gift from your dear ninety-year-old Aunt Erma. Only problem is, you don't decorate in purple and you didn't need any towels. What do you do? Give them back to Aunt Erma? Ask for a receipt to take them back? Both would be kind of awkward, and that's where "regifting" comes in. Okay, you've heard of recycling, but what is regifting? It's exactly what it sounds like—you store that gift and then give it to someone else when the occasion arises. That, of course, solves the problem just mentioned, plus it saves you money at gift-buying time. That's big. And should you think it's uncouth, according to regiftable.com, two out of three people have either regifted or considered regifting. So don't need or want those windmill salt and pepper shakers you got for Mother's Day? Give them to Aunt Erma.

Gift shopping? Make a list and stick to it.

Being organized always helps when it comes to money. But nowhere is that more important than when it comes to gift shopping. Especially during the December holidays, retailers hope that while you're cruising the aisles, you'll see a few more "perfect gift ideas" for little Jonnie and Uncle George—and a few things you just have to have for yourself. Soon, any notion of a gift "budget" is out the window and spending is out of control. So do just like Santa did in the old days—make a list and check it twice. P.S. This works for other kinds of shopping expeditions, like your weekly trip to the grocery.

A picture can be worth a thousand bucks.

People feel compelled to buy "stuff" for gifts, especially at the holidays. But most of us have too much "stuff" anyway and don't need more—who really needs the latest bread machine, anyway? What many people love instead is a really good picture of something important. Consider giving a picture of your family or other people that are special to them—maybe their own family in a special place or on a special trip you took together. So take pictures of your family and friends—and get one printed up, maybe with a nice inscription, or the place and date, and put it in a nice frame. There you go. Family pictures make great greeting cards, too—we've been making our own Mother's Day cards with family photos for years.

Save containers to mail gifts.

If you mail a lot of gifts, costs can add up in a hurry. Not only do you pay rather hefty shipping costs, but you'll also dole out a lot for containers, packaging, and packing services, too. If you can, it's a good idea to keep a few shipping boxes on hand somewhere—maybe one or two of those small Amazon boxes, maybe one or two larger. Keep the inflatable wraps and bubble wraps too. When gift time comes around, you'll be glad you did. And here's an even better way to save on shipping and packaging costs: Use gift cards. They aren't for everyone—people like the notion of getting something picked out especially for them. But others on your list, especially children, love the power and freedom of picking something out themselves.

Shipping stuff? Shop for the cheapest way in advance.

You're down to the wire for sending something—maybe a holiday gift package—to someone somewhere. You give up and decide just to take it to the post office. Yikes! Forty-five bucks to ship that thirty dollar gift! It can happen. That's why it's best to research the alternatives in advance, either by going to the Web sites of specific carriers, dropping in on one of your local "Pak Mail" or similar shipping outlets, or trying out your shipment on uship.com's shipping cost estimator at www.uship.com/price_estimator.aspx. (This site has a lot of other helpful advice, too). And before you haul that hockey set for the grandkids to UPS, make sure you pack it efficiently. You might think the carrier likes super-thick, super-safe packaging—but the reality is much of that packing material is air; it takes up a lot of space, and they may charge you more for it (it's called dimensional weight). So before you mark a rush on your shipping endeavors, do a little homework and plan your best route.

"Inflation is when you pay fifteen dollars for the ten-dollar haircut you used to get for five dollars when you had hair."

—Sam Ewing

Take and bake your meals at home.

Grocery stores and a certain few franchises have picked up on the fact that people can't afford to eat out all the time, but don't have time for all that cooking and cleanup, either. So, enter the ready-made meal—ready-made for your oven, that is. As an example, many groceries have "take-and-bake" pizzas—ready to stick in the oven; the chain Papa Murphy's also specializes in this. You get a really good product for half the price of a pizzeria, plus you can do the baking part at home while you dispose of the day's junk mail and help Frankie with his homework. Some restaurants, also seeing this trend, are starting to offer full carryout meals, cooked and ready to go. You don't save as much as if you heat it up yourself, but you'll save the tip, and you'll save sales tax in the many states that consider a carryout meal as non-taxable "food" rather than a restaurant meal.

Make your favorite restaurant meal at home.

This idea, of course, won't work for everything—most of us don't know how to make a soufflé and don't want to mess with Beef Wellington because of time, fear of failure, and cost of those really special ingredients. But if your favorite restaurant meal is prime rib or something like that, you can save a bundle. A prime rib dinner for two at the local steakhouse will set you back at least $70 and usually more (especially if you bring the kids). But we've found you can buy that same roast for $25 to $35—sometimes less during the holidays—and do it yourself. It isn't that hard. Decorate the table with flowers, get out the tablecloth and linen napkins, and enjoy a restaurant-grade meal at home.

Buy real food, not the stuff in boxes.

Convenience is king these days, we know, and we use a lot of prepared packaged and frozen foods just to keep things going on a busy evening. But if you learn to use basic foods instead, you can save; besides fresh foods are healthier. Real potatoes, for instance, are good for you, still pretty darned cheap, and boiling and mashing them doesn't take long. We're surprised at how many people have forgotten how to cook real potatoes and instead use dried flakes or frozen bags instead! And vegetables—skip the boiling bag stuff and use the basic frozen varieties (which were the "fancy" versions fifty years ago) or better, choose fresh-produce alternatives, like Brussels sprouts or corn.

Reevaluate your insurance—all of it.

Most people hate buying insurance. Lots of dough for something that (hopefully) you'll never really need. So they buy a few policies (more precisely, they are sold a few policies) and they go on their merry way—for years. But needs change and costs change. For instance, because of increased life expectancy, did you know that most life insurance policies have gone down in price for the last ten years? Sit down with a qualified, trustworthy insurance agent, or even a financial adviser, for a full review of your insurance. You may or may not save money at day's end, but you're more likely to spend your hard-earned insurance dollars on the coverage you really need.

Buy term life insurance.

Life insurance companies have perpetually sought ways to get more money out of their clients and build longer-term relationships. And life insurance salespeople have perpetually sought ways to get the highest possible commissions. Both practices have led to the creation of so-called "permanent" insurance forms, where you buy a product with both an insurance value and an investment value. So-called whole life, universal life, and variable universal life are all forms of permanent insurance. Unfortunately, for the most part, when you get investment "value" it takes away from the pure purpose of the insurance—to protect you—and it costs more. The "product" can't be best at two things at once. Insurance companies have proven better over the years at managing their investments than managing yours—you won't hear too many people crow about "beating the market" with their insurance policies, right? So our advice is to keep it simple and just buy the term insurance you need—a simple premium for a simple dollar-amount insurance coverage through a simple date. Leave all that complicated stuff for someone else.

Avoid "free trials."

Getting something for free always sounds appealing, but be warned about anything that offers a "free trial." Better Business Bureaus are kept busy with complaints about free trials that weren't, from consumers who can't get through to a company when they try to cancel and can't stop the automatic credit-card charge. This is a situation you don't want to be in, so don't put yourself in it.

Frugal funerals are OK.

Death happens, and burial can be costly. It is such an emotional time that it can be hard to make the right decisions about how much to spend. Never allow a funeral home to "guilt" you into spending more than you want on a coffin, or spending the money on embalming (at a cost of around $3,000) if skipping the embalming and having a closed coffin is fine with you. If you feel pressured, try another funeral home.

Check out the information at the Funeral Consumers Alliance, www.funerals.org, for information on how and where (it is illegal in some states) you can handle the arrangements yourself.

Skip the diet miracles.

The ads pop up every time you go online, or every time you open a magazine. Diet Miracle! Recommended by Oprah! Miracle Weight Loss Cure! They can be convincing . . .

Save your money and skip the persuasive promises. Diet miracles are hype, and very expensive hype at that. So skip them all. You don't need powders, you don't need pills, and you don't need special drinks. If you want to lose weight the miracle formula is simple—eat less and exercise more.

Don't block heating and A/C vents.

Your furnace and air conditioner work hard to regulate the temperature in your house. So why would you put a big piece of furniture or a rug over your vents? Doing so will make the system work harder, make more air come out in the wrong places (creating drafts), and create warm or cold spots in the house. Make sure nothing is on top of—or in front of—those vents. And don't forget the cold air return, that big "vent" that sucks air into the system—that one's got to be free to breathe, too.

Don't get steered into a bar.

Going out to eat? Nice. Especially if you aren't in a hurry and have time to enjoy the peace and quiet away from the kids, away from the stresses of the world. But wait—you walk into the restaurant. Yeah, it's busy, but there are tables here and there, and yet, what do they do? They ask "Would you like to sit in the bar until your table's ready?" Of course, they may truly be full, but their intent may also be to help you run up a bar tab. If the restaurant isn't really full, that's probably the case. So, opt to walk around outside for some fresh air for a while, or if it's six degrees below, sit in a waiting area, but don't be tempted to go into the bar. You'll have plenty of time for that drink at your table, and it's better with your meal, anyway. Come to think of it, the best way to avoid this budget buster is to only go to restaurants that take reservations.

Set up a household clean team.

Keeping a house clean is a daunting task, especially for busy people. The overwhelming temptation is to farm out the job, but that can cost $40 a week and up. So organize your family unit into a "clean team." Everyone gets a task, everyone gets together, say, from 10:00 to 11:00 on Saturday morning, to blitzkrieg the house. Make it fun with time challenges (how fast can so-and-so clean a toilet?) and fill it full of rewards—maybe a little cash spread around the house, maybe a fun meal afterwards. It can be entertaining and productive, and best of all, you'll end up with a clean house.

Buy gas on Tuesdays.

It may hardly be noticeable, but those who study these things have concluded that gas prices are most expensive on weekends, when most working folks have time for errands and they're taking their road trips. Buy gas midweek, and it may be cheaper. Same goes for gas in the spring and fall. The summer driving season drives prices up routinely, while cold winters can create energy shortages. Think about that when planning your vacation. And even if the gauge isn't on empty, if it's Tuesday, it may be time to head to the pumps.

Check your gas cap.

Of course, most states and areas with emissions testing laws will take care of this for you with inspection programs, but know that gas just loves to evaporate into thin air and will do so quite willingly at the sign of a missing or poorly fitting gas cap. These devices cost under $10. Studies show that 20 percent of all cars have some sort of gas-cap problem, and that some 147 million gallons become vapor each year as a result. That's a lotta gas.

Combine your errands—follow the rule of three.

High gas prices and long commutes have made a lot of us smarter about combining trips, but not as smart as we could be. Still, more than one quarter of all car trips are under a mile, and many people are still prone to do their errands, pick up the kids, and so on, one at a time. That's a lot of trips, a lot of wasted gas, and a lot of wasted time. So here's an idea—don't go anywhere unless you can accomplish at least three things on your trip. Oh, of course, there will be some exceptions to that, else your little Andrea will have to spend the night after her basketball practice. But you get the idea. Plan ahead. You'll save money and time.

Park where the sun don't shine.

Gas really likes to evaporate, and get it warm inside your tank and fuel lines, and it will go anywhere it can. That includes out the gas filler and gas cap (see the tip above) and out through the fuel injection or carburetor system in your engine compartment. And when your car gets hot, it only wants to get out all that much more. So if you can avoid it, don't park your car in hot sun—look for a shady spot. You'll be more comfortable when you get in the car, and your interior will last longer, too.

Know when to—and when not to—use your car's A/C.

You've heard that running the air conditioner makes your engine work harder—and use more gas. For the most part, this is true. So naturally, the instinct is to, when possible, turn off the A/C and open the windows. Good instinct— but it isn't always right. The problem is that today's modern cars are designed to run with the A/C on. Why? Because of aerodynamics—open windows actually create drag at higher speeds. So you're actually better—above 40 mph—to keep the A/C on.

Sign up for "Ding."

Want cheap air travel? There are a lot of ways to find it online. But one of the most straightforward and dependable ways to keep tabs on the bargains is to sign up for the airline's own specials. Why? Because they are tuned "real time" to the inventory of bookings and empty seats available. Most airlines, if you sign up, will send you "e-fares" and other bargains. The familiar "Ding" signals alerts arriving from Southwest Airlines.

Discover the least expensive airports.

Want to fly to Cincinnati? Easy to do, but you'll pay through the nose. Why? Because the service is dominated by Delta Airlines, which uses the city as a hub, and it has an outsized proportion of business travelers. So how does one get to Cincy cheap? Fly to the more competitive Indianapolis or Dayton or Columbus, rent a car, and drive. The couple hundred for the rental will be more than offset by the airfare savings. This works in other places too—Manchester, New Hampshire, is cheaper than Boston; Providence, Rhode Island, is also cheaper than Boston and most places in Connecticut. Also, check out Baltimore to get to places farther down the coast. In fact, you could start by checking out where discounters Southwest Airlines or JetBlue fly.

Go postal.

Using FedEx and UPS seems like the businesslike way to go with your important mail, but those delivery fees add up to real money. Instead of the costly delivery services, use the good old American postal service. You will save around $20 by opting to send mail second-day "priority" delivery with the USPS. And remember that by planning ahead and not procrastinating, you can avoid sending anything in a rush.

Send e-cards.

Avoid spending money on gift cards and postage by sending out e-cards instead. There are many sites to choose from, from www.hallmark.com to www.care2.com. Using Care2 not only saves you money on cards, but gives money to charity for each card you send, so you are "doing good" while you save money.

"If you want to know what a man is really like, take notice of how he acts when he loses money."

—Simone Weil

One dollar saved is equal to two dollars earned.

How much is money really worth? Even more than you'd think, once you realize how long it takes to earn it. A dollar is a dollar, right? Nope. That dollar you are about to drop on a candy bar actually used to be around $2 when you worked for it, but after all those pesky taxes were taken out you ended up with the dollar you are about to spend. Think about it. So whenever you opt not to spend money, consider that it's twice as valuable to you and your time and effort.

Give a poem.

The most meaningful gift of all is free. Write a poem or a letter or create a CD or an iPod directory expressing your own thoughts to share with a loved one or a friend. It is more valuable than any expensive trinket could ever be.

Extend your juice.

Juice is costly. So in order to make your juice dollars go further, just add water. Once your juice carton is at least one-third empty, go ahead and add plain tap water and shake to blend. With most kinds of juices you won't even notice, and they will last 30 percent longer for the same price.

Limit kids' TV viewing.

Just as research has shown that watching sitcoms set in upscale homes (and the commercials that accompany them) can influence adults to overspend, children's desires can be easily influenced by commercial television. If they don't watch the shows with ads for expensive toys and breakfast cereals, they won't know that stuff exists, and they won't ask you to buy it for them.

Celebrate homemade holidays.

Instead of buying holiday decorations, spend a crafty afternoon with your children and make your own. Cardboard and tin foil can be turned into Christmas stars for your windows, old sheets can become Halloween ghosts, and a walk outdoors will give you the chance to gather up plenty of autumn leaves for Thanksgiving table decorations.

Rewind your fax cartridge.

A thrifty approach to making a fax-machine cartridge last longer is to simply rewind it once it has reached the end of the spool. It is a tedious procedure, but it can be done. If you rewind the film you can use the same cartridge two or three times. This adds up to big savings.

Check your restaurant bills.

Always check what you have been charged for before paying the bill. No one is out to cheat you, but sometimes an errant charge or a double charge can appear. Jennifer recently noticed an extra $1.50 charge on a bill for a simple soup lunch. "Extra bread," the waitress explained. "Those two tiny croutons floating in my soup?" Jennifer disagreed, and the charge was removed.

Stop looking in the mirror.

So much of our spending goes towards improving our own images, so what if we just stopped looking in the mirror so often? We would all obsess less about our aging faces (and save money on cosmetics and wrinkle creams), less about our hair (and save money on cuts and color), and less about our outfits (and save money on clothes and accessories). The architect Frank Gehry observed at his eightieth birthday party, "I don't feel 80. I guess you never think you're the age you are, and, as long as you don't look in the mirror, you aren't."

Plant a money garden.

With an eye towards increased interest in vegetable gardening, the Burpee Seed Company, www.burpee.com, has developed a "Money Garden" seed packet. Six different kinds of vegetables are included for $10. The company says the plants will produce $650 dollars worth of produce.

Freelance your way to savings.

Perhaps you have some talent as a freelance writer, reporter, or journalist. Perhaps you do a lot of writing on your current job, or maybe once worked on the high school yearbook, newspaper—or if you're under thirty—on the school Web site or blog. If you can put together a few hundred words of decent writing, you might not only be able to make a few dollars selling your work, but you could save a lot too. How? Businesses of all types crave publicity, especially free publicity. You create the publicity, and all they have to do is turn you on to their product or service. It can even be for your own company newsletter. So write about someone's restaurant and get the piece placed, even for free, and you might get a free dinner out of it. It doesn't hurt to set your sights high; it's possible to get "comped" a night or even more at a lot of first-class hotels and restaurants.

No impulse buys. Ever!

You see it all the time in groceries. As you move your cart up to the cashier, a wall of little goodies up and down both sides. Candy, magazines, cute little books about what to name your kid or how to lose weight or win at Sudoku—all there for your eyeballs to take in while you wait. Why? Simple—the store wants to squeeze a few more dollars out of you. It's pretty obvious in groceries and a bit more subtle in other stores, but make no mistake, all want to capture the impulse buy. So what to do? Don't give in to impulse. If something catches your eye (or your kids' eyes) that wasn't part of the shopping plan, just say no. Period.

Fix the faucet drips.

A leaky faucet can waste hundreds of gallons every year. If it's cold water, it won't cost a lot (a toilet, however, can cost a lot more). But if it's hot water, that's a different story. That leaky faucet can cost 800, maybe 1,000 gallons of hot water a year—twenty or thirty tankfuls. That can translate into sizable energy costs. How to fix the problem? Just enter "fix a leaky faucet" in your search engine; you'll find a lot of tips. One of the more user-friendly approaches comes from the "Handy Ma'am" section of the iVillage Web site (http://home.ivillage.com/homeimprovement/fixit/0,,8t4c,00.html). An added bonus: You won't have to listen to the "drip, drip, drip" any longer.

"Economy is half the battle of life: it is not so hard to earn money as it is to spend it well."

—C. H. Spurgeon

Make your fresh cut flowers last longer.

Flowers are great. They spruce up a room and make you feel better about it. But they don't last long, do they? Replacing them every few days could cost a bundle. So here's what to do (outside of getting those silk flowers, which are nice but expensive and not the real thing). Put a penny in the water, or even aspirin, or even ice! The biology or chemistry may be complicated, but the result is simple: it works.

Pay off credit card bills every month.

It goes without saying that spending only what you earn and can afford to pay off every month is a good idea. You'll save not only the interest (a lot—$15 to $25 a month or so for every $1,000 carried over on your card), but you'll get a better credit rating, which will lead to lower borrowing costs later. If you have the discipline to pay off every month, you have the discipline to pay on time—so you'll save on late and default fees, too. Most importantly, if you make monthly payoff your rule, you'll spend less—because you know you'll have to pay the piper sooner rather than later.

Autopay? Proceed with caution.

Paying your bills automatically every month is probably a good idea for the relatively undisciplined or inexperienced personal financier. Why? Because it saves late fees, credit dings, and a variety of other expensive ills associated with credit cards. But do so with care—it's easy to forget to examine your statements when autopay is in place, and everyone should examine statements to check for errors and to get more clues as to how they spend money each month. So yes, autopay can save fees and interest (and postage, too), but make sure you look at your statements in the mail or online anyway, and make sure to set up some kind of overdraft protection for your account.

Make loan payments using direct payment.

Many installment loans, like car loans, and even some mortgages. will offer better rates—perhaps as much as a quarter of a percent—if you make the payment automatically from a checking or some other account. Now, auto bill pay has its hazards, for you need to monitor your statements regularly to catch errors and unexpected expenses, and autopay makes it easy for you to postpone or even avoid that necessary oversight. But the situation is different with an installment loan. The payment is the same every month, so no problems there. So check out direct payment savings—it might not be available for loans outstanding, but it's worth asking about for any future loans.

Sweeten your own cereal.

In this era of prepackaged cereals, most of us have gotten into the habit of simply pouring the cereal in a bowl, pouring the milk on top, and on with the show. But you can save by adding your own sweets. If you like raisin bran, try starting with corn flakes or Wheaties and adding your own raisins. Or simply add sugar to Cheerios or corn flakes. The package price may not be cheaper, but that package holding unsweetened cereal is usually quite a bit bigger than the one holding its sweetened counterpart. Here's another idea from our own kitchen: Take ordinary shredded wheat (full-sized), spread peanut butter on it, then add sugar, and then milk. You'll wonder how anyone ate shredded wheat any other way.

Find other ways to cook.

Sure, it's easiest to cook lunch or dinner on the primary stove or range or in the oven in your kitchen. But especially if these appliances are electric, the energy use isn't trivial, especially over the long run. An hour with an electric oven can cost 30 cents to a dollar depending on temperature and rates; that might not seem like much, but it adds up. You'll save by using the outdoor grill every now and then or even an electric skillet or toaster oven.

Buy a small freezer.

A small 5- to 7-cubic-foot chest freezer might cost $175 to $250 at a discount retailer, plus you'll spend energy to run it. But if you plan your purchases, you can save a lot, sometimes 50 percent or more, by buying large quantities of meat and other items. But you have to plan; otherwise, the stuff disappears into the frozen depths of the freezer not to surface for years. Especially if you have a large family, run the numbers.

Price insurance alternatives online.

For many reasons, online has become a place to buy so many things. It's fast, it's easy, you don't have to go anywhere, you can learn a lot about the product, it's easy to compare prices, and you can "disintermediate" the middlemen in many cases. The last two reasons especially make it sensible to shop for insurance online. Insurance is sold by salespeople, and those salespeople make a lot in commissions. Even if you want to ultimately buy from a salesperson because you're not sure what to buy or how different policies work (both situations are not uncommon), the Internet is a great way to "pre-shop" the sale so you know what's out there and what it costs. Take test drives on esurance.com, ehealthinsurance.com, insweb .com, and lowestpolicy.com.

.

Work at home—at least one day a week.

We know it isn't possible for all of you to work where you want to, whether that's home, Starbucks, or your in-laws' plush library. But if you can arrange to work at home even one day a week, you could save 20 percent of your commute costs, assuming you work a five-day week, and maybe a lunch out. Also, you might get more work done because you don't have any distractions. It could be a win-win—if your boss sees it that way. Of course, if you're a surgical nurse or an air traffic controller, we know it just plain won't work, but hey, there are 572 other tips here for you.

Cut back weekly and monthly services.

When times are great and we seem to have more income than we can spend, and our assets are growing by leaps and bounds too, we get things taken care of without worrying too much about the cost. Have a few ants? Get a monthly pest control service. Don't want to dust or clean windows? Hire a weekly cleaning service. But now you're spending $50 to $75 a month for the pest control and maybe $200 a month for the cleaning service, not to mention other services. Are we saying cut the services off completely? No. Just consider cutting back. Perhaps pest control every other month. Perhaps a cleaning service every other week. You can always order out the pest control guy when the ants attack—and when they don't, you'll save.

Cell phones for the family? Make them similar or the same.

It may be harder than it sounds, but if everyone in the family has the same or a similar cell phone, you'll save on chargers and accessories, and it'll be easier for people to share them or borrow one from another if one is lost or breaks. All you have to do, with some major carriers anyway, is change the so-called "SIM" card and another family member can use it right away.

Order sandwiches—not entrees.

Go to a restaurant and order a steak, and it probably will cost $25 or so. Go to the same restaurant and order a steak sandwich, and it will cost $11.95. Sure, it's not quite as big, but with that nice Kaiser roll underneath it, who's to notice? The same idea applies to prime rib, some kinds of fish, chicken, and other entrees. Or, if you're just plain in a penny-pinching mood, order the burger or a nice grilled ham-and-cheese sandwich. In most places you'll be just as full and just as happy as if you ordered the big meal.

Try a doc-in-the-box.

"Doc-in-the-box" is slang for one of the many hundreds of retail medical clinics going up across the country under the name "Med Clinic" or something similar. They aren't places to get diagnosis or treatment for serious diseases, but if you or your kids need an antibiotic prescription or have a sports injury or need a flu shot or a sports physical—that is, routine medical care—they work pretty well. For one thing, they have extended hours into the evenings or weekends; for another, they can handle you on a walk-in basis with little to no wait and will save you 10, 20 or as much as 50 percent in cost, not to mention your savings in time and aggravation. They're especially good if you have a high-deductible or high co-pay health plan.

Wanna golf? Play twilight.

So you want a full-day outing with the boys, eighteen holes and nothing less? Fine. Be prepared to pay $40 to $400 depending on whether it's the Mainstreet Muni or Pebble Beach. But want to save some bucks, and don't care if you only get thirteen holes in? Play twilight. Most courses go to twilight pricing three or four hours before dark. You'll get the golf in, the course won't be too crowded, and you'll save maybe half. And the nineteenth hole is still open for a burger and a beer afterward.

Avoid fancy-branded athletic wear.

Need a pair of running shoes? Athletic warm-ups? Socks? Sure, you can buy those Nikes or Under Armours or New Balance, but you'll pay more, a lot more in many cases. Keep in mind that the lesser-known brands may work well too. Heck, a lot of them are made in the same overseas factories. So don't get so caught up in the brands. Still, if you're really in love with that pair of Nike running shorts or shoes, wait for the new styles to come in, like they always do, and you might catch what you want on sale.

Buy your golf stuff before you hit the course.

It's a beautiful Saturday, and you and the girls have waited for weeks for clear weather and clear calendars. And now it's finally here. Dust off those clubs, show up an hour early to hit some balls—a perfect day. But wait, the golf bag is empty— no tees, no balls, no visor, no towel. Pretty soon you've gone through $50 or so for this "stuff" at full golf-course prices— all added into the greens fees, cart fees, and lunch. Makes for a pretty expensive day. Plan ahead, shop ahead, and make it a point to hit that discount golf or sporting goods or heck— Kmart—the Friday evening before the round. This sort of planning helps with other sports, like skiing, boating, etc. too. You plan ahead for your kids' sports. Why not your own?

Bring a sandwich.

Going on a hike? Skiing? Playing a round of golf? Headed out to who-knows-where with some buddies? Take a sandwich. You'll avoid restaurants, particularly the expensive sort you'll typically find at ski resorts and the like. Again, a little preparation can save a lot of dough over the course of a year. These days, your buddies will even think you're smart.

"The glow of one warm thought is to me worth more than money."

—Thomas Jefferson

Have a not-so-big wedding.

Weddings don't have to be big, expensive affairs, in fact, the most personal of all are quite modest in size and scale. Read how one couple did a smallish and budget-minded wedding spending just $2,000, on www.2000wedding.com. You can also get money-saving tips from the Offbeat Bride at www.offbeatbride.com.

Reuse old gold.

It is hard to find well-priced gold rings nowadays, so one way to save money on wedding rings is to have your family donate their unused gold jewelry to Green Karat, www.greenkarat.com, where it will be made into new jewelry for you and your intended.

Reuse vacuum cleaner bags.

Okay, this does sound desperate, but trust us, it works. Jennifer has done it several times successfully, and has not only saved herself the price of a package of vacuum cleaner bags, but also saved the extra trip to the store where you just know she would have bought two or three other things! How do you reuse a vacuum cleaner bag? Simple, just open it at the bottom, shake it thoroughly over a garbage can (she recommends doing it outdoors; it is a dusty business) and then refold the bottom and staple it in several places.

"Creditors have better memories than debtors."

—Benjamin Franklin

Use Katie's money-saving grocery method.

Katie Schardt used to plan out her week's menus, draw up a list of ingredients she needed, and then shop for them at the local grocery store. "I thought it was the most efficient way to do it. And then I discovered a Grocery Outlet store and changed my method completely." Katie now does her meal planning in reverse. She goes to the discount grocer, buys the meat that is on sale, and then plans her meals around that. "I've cut my grocery bill in half," she told us.

Put it out there.

Need something in your life but can't afford it right now? No sense keeping that information to yourself. Put it out there and let everyone know what you are looking for. You never know. Maybe they have what you need and would be willing to give it to you or trade for it. Our friend Cathleen used to keep a list posted by her front door of the things she needed. An ironing board. Help with her garden. Inner tubes for her bike. Whenever someone was on their way out her door they would see the list, and low and behold, many friends stopped and said, "Oh, you need that? I've got one you can have."

Visit Venice in the winter.

One of the world's most desirable locations is much more affordable in the wintertime. Matt Gross, the Frugal Traveler for the *New York Times,* recently recommended going at that time of the year, getting low-season hotel rates, and buying a VeniceCard that is good for free entry into many of the museums and churches. You can get a VeniceCard at www. helloVenezia.com.

When in doubt—clean.

Before you decide to replace something, why not clean it instead? Shine up that old coffee pot, dust off the bookcases, and send the drapes to the cleaners instead of heading out to buy new ones. You might just find there is plenty of life left in the things you already own.

D-I-Y Caesar salad.

A deliciously affordable indulgence is a Caesar salad, made from scratch. Sure, it costs $10 in a restaurant, but the ingredients themselves don't cost much. Lettuce, eggs, garlic, olive oil, Parmesan cheese—you probably have those things now. Old bread to make some croutons. And then a tin of anchovies, which should cost less than $1 at the store. Check out this simple recipe at www.reluctantgourmet.com/caesar.htm. Once you learn how to treat yourself at home with this inexpensive recipe, you will never again order it in a restaurant.

Create a new look.

Stay out of the furniture and home décor stores and spend an afternoon moving your own furniture around. Create a whole new look with what you have. Drape a shawl over the worn part of the couch, bring some pillows from the bedroom into the living room, and trade lamps from another part of the house. You might find that you didn't really need to buy anything new; you were just tired of the way the room looked.

Pause for a better deal.

You've found what you want online, put it in the virtual shopping cart, now the best thing to do is . . . wait. Leave it in your online cart, but don't complete the purchase. A survey from an online commerce consulting group found that in many cases this action triggered a follow-up email offering a further discount.

Make your own play dough.

Stop buying your children the commercially produced molding clay, and make it yourself for far less. Ask them to help you make it, and the afternoon will be even more fun! You can find several recipes for making your own play dough (including a recipe that uses peanut butter) at the TeachNet Web site, www.teachnet.com/lesson/art/playdoughrecipes/traditional.html.

Entertain with brunch.

Not only is splurging on brunch a less costly way to enjoy a restaurant meal, but entertaining at home with a brunch is far less expensive than a dinner party. Bake up bread and coffee cakes, offer up an egg-based main dish like frittata, put out some fruit salad, and put the coffee pot on. You and your friends will enjoy a relaxed and low-pressure afternoon.

Save on European rental cars.

Keep the costs of a European trip even lower by not renting a car for the entire time, but only for short periods when you need it. Hertz now is offering a Hertz369 program in several countries that lets you rent a car for just three hours, or six hours, or nine. Look on www.hertz.com for information and details.

Another option in London and Paris is a car-sharing program that rents a fleet of Mini Coopers and Ford Fiestas. You pay an annual membership fee, and then an hourly rate, starting at $5.12 per hour. Find out about it at www.connect byhertz.com.

Have drinks in a grand hotel.

Staying at a bargain hotel but still want to have a bit of luxury in your life? Dress up and go and have drinks at the fancy bar in town. No need to be a hotel guest to enjoy drinks at the Plaza in New York, the Ritz in Paris, or The Empress in Vancouver, B.C. For the price of a drink you can relax and enjoy the atmosphere without having to pop for the high-priced room.

Be a flexible flyer.

Suppose you need to go to New York on Monday July 1, morning arrival, non-stop, return after 5:00 p.m. Friday. Sure, you can do that. But be prepared to pay a lot for the privilege. Airlines know that business travelers like the prime schedules, and can usually afford to pay for them. Now, suppose you need to be in New York for something. If you can fly Tuesday, arrive late in the evening, make a stopover, or fly into nearby Newark or even Allentown, Pennsylvania, you might save a bundle. Most airline and travel sites make it easy to see how much you can save if you can change the dates, times, and routes just a little bit. Learn how to use these features. Get used to using the "flexible dates" feature on, for instance, the Kayak travel search engine at www.kayak.com.

Fly Tuesday, Wednesday, Saturday.

To get the best deals, plan your trips for these three days. Why? Because business travelers prefer Sunday, Monday, Thursday, and Friday, of course. Not only will you save a bunch, but your flight will be a lot less crowded, too. Beyond that, mid-morning flights tend to be the cheapest. So if you're planning a weeklong vacation, leave Saturday, come back Wednesday, and spend a few days enjoying your home and garden.

Take two trips for the price of one.

The airlines introduced cheap round-trip "super-saver" fares more than thirty years ago—you know, the ones where you have to book two weeks in advance, stay a Saturday night, and keep it to a simple round-trip. Well, now the rules are relaxed to the point that you need to purchase in advance, but not more than that. Many airlines, like Southwest, offer cheap fares for single legs—you can fly from Sacramento to Phoenix, then Denver, then back to Sacramento, all at the best prices subject to availability. So now you can go where you want to go—and combine two trips into one. So go visit Grandma in Phoenix, then hit the slopes in Winter Park for a few days—and save money compared to two separate trips.

Make your own insecticide.

You can spend a lot on insecticides, including the price you pay in possible health damage and environmental costs too. But you can also make your own witches brew of ten cloves of garlic, a tablespoon of vegetable oil, three cups of hot water and a teaspoon of dish soap. Yes, it sort of sounds like what you'd find in your sink along with your soaking dishes after a rich Italian meal. But it works.

Make your own spot weed killer.

Sure, Roundup works great, but it costs a bundle, especially if you just need a little, because you have to buy a lot, even in the smaller containers. So try making a mix of your own: Blend 2 cups of liquid bleach in 1 gallon of hot water.

Make mine a wrap.

There are hundreds of ways to satisfy those food cravings, especially the ones your young ones bring home from school at the end of the day. Sure, you can stock bread, mayonnaise and all the goodies you need to make sandwiches, but it's expensive and the bread doesn't stay good forever. So learn to do it the tortilla way—you can take leftovers or eggs or meat scraps or bits of sandwich meat with some leftover rice—or—you name it—and make a wrap out of it. it's a great, simple way to use what you have and package and serve it in a way you and your kids will enjoy.

Be a smart prescription buyer.

Especially if you have to take medications regularly, the cost of prescriptions can really add up, even if you have great insurance coverage. So if you need that indomethacin anti-inflammatory or lovastatin for cholesterol, you can buy a thirty-day supply for four bucks. In fact, at Walmart and now many competing retailers, you can buy over 1,000 different medicines for $4 for a thirty-days supply and $10 for a ninety-day supply. And here's another idea, used for years by seniors on a tight budget—cut your pills in half. If you get a prescription with twice the strength and half the quantity, it often costs less, and insurance co-pays will be less. Then simply split the pills. Talk to your doctor and pharmacist.

Just try rest.

Under the weather? Sick with a cold or flu? Here's one old-fashioned medication that really works—just stay home and rest. Many of us are so determined to deal with the symptoms and carry on with our lives that we end up taxing our bodies even more; then our illness gets worse and lasts longer. So to get better faster and save money on doctor visits and all those symptom control medications, simply sleep in for a day. Your body can do wonderful things when it gets a chance, and resting your brain for a while isn't a bad thing, either.

Need medicine? Get samples.

Drug companies really lay it on to the medical, dental, optometric, and other health care providers to get them to sell their products. As a result, most docs have a room full of samples ready and waiting to give to patients who might be in need—samples of medications, the latest floss pick, or even contact lens solutions and cases. So, just like taking the shampoo and conditioner home from the hotels, take advantage of what's there. When you go to the doc, ask! You might be surprised by what they have to offer.

Take your shoes off.

If you travel to Asia, it's customary to take off your shoes when you enter someone's home. It's considered polite, not to mention cleaner, quieter, and more relaxing, to go around in socks. Those on this side of the Pacific, particularly with carpets and rugs in our homes, know this custom keeps carpets cleaner and nicer longer too. Longer lasting carpets and fewer carpet cleanings will save you money. And by the way, the sock rule prohibits not just shoes, but also bare feet.

You pack. They drive.

An alternative to hiring an expensive professional moving company is to use a new type of service. Going the high-priced route, you'd have a crew show up, pack your stuff in the truck, and drive it to your new place to unload it. But with MoveAmerica (www.moveamerica.com) or Help-U-Move (http://helpumove.com), you can bring the cost down by doing the packing yourself. These companies deliver a 28-foot trailer to your house and leave it there for you to pack yourself. When you are done and ready to move, they will come back, hitch it up again, and professional drivers will take care of getting the truck across town or across the country. It ends up costing about half the price of hiring the professional movers.

No need for expensive wedding gifts.

Just because you have been invited to a wedding doesn't mean you are obligated to buy an expensive gift. From an etiquette point of view, the only wedding event that requires a gift is a bridal shower. The wedding invitation itself comes with no strings attached.

So if there isn't room in your budget for a gift, don't feel guilty. Go ahead and attend; that is why they invited you.

Need college spending money? Work for the school.

The cost of college is high enough just counting the expected stuff—tuition, room, board. But what about all those other expenses normally filed under the category of "spending money?" Beer money, pizza money, gas money, and so on? One way to cut the cost of college is to work for the school. Undergraduate students can earn that spending money and sometimes even the cost of room and board by becoming an "R.A.," or resident advisor, in a dorm. Graduate students can become graduate assistants, perhaps to help a professor with a project or program. Both help defray costs, and the R.A. job in particular is an excellent way to gain maturity and preparation for responsibilities that will come with adult life.

"The art is not in making money, but in keeping it."

—Proverb

Learn how stores code sale prices.

The best way to save money is to not buy anything. The second best way to save money is to buy stuff on sale. That's why it's important to watch for sales and for sale-priced items. Most stores do a pretty good job of letting you know what's on sale—when they really want to or have the time. Signs, special floor locations, blue light specials—you name it. But sometimes cues are more subtle—in part because not every store has the time, energy, space, nor the agility to put "sale" signs on everything. Items move on and off sale too fast. So it helps to learn how the store marks stuff on sale for its own employees. It might be a different colored shelf tag at the grocery. It might be a price that ends in a ".99" or even a ".93" or a ".43" whereas most prices are in round figures. Look closely at the shelves—or ask a clerk if you get a chance.

You can negotiate your medical bills.

When most of us hear something from someone in the medical field—a diagnosis, a recommendation for a test—we have a tendency to treat it as gospel. And that includes the bill for services rendered. As it turns out, there may be room to negotiate some parts of a bill. For instance, if you're having two dental crowns done, the dentist may pass on some of the savings of doing it with only one appointment and even one anesthetic. As it turns out, according to one study, 60 to 70 percent of patients who negotiate their hospital bills receive a discount. Bottom line: it never hurts to ask.

Make yourself a guinea pig.

Small businesses and professionals everywhere look for "reference accounts." A reference account is an account or client they can count on for referrals when they go looking for other clients. You become an example of a good service performed, or a new service performed, for that business. So if you have some great fancy new water feature added to your backyard, talk to your contractor about a small discount for giving him the privilege of showing your house to other potential clients. It may not work, but it doesn't hurt to ask.

Try an agritourism vacation.

Especially when economic times are tough, we all think about getting back to our roots. That can mean anything from visiting our families to visiting our old family homes. For many of us it can also mean getting back to our agrarian roots: 50 percent or more of us, after all, can trace our ancestry back to the farm. Now there is little that's more genuine, nor important, than working hard to grow food. And a trip to the farm serves well to make us more aware of what goes into food and the importance of agriculture. What's more, a trip to the farm is a short and inexpensive trip, and it inspires awareness of basic foods, which in turn might produce a better-for-your-budget change in eating habits. Agritourism has become a new back-to-basics travel movement—check out www.agritourismworld.com, or for a specific example, check out Anne Dougherty's Learn Great Foods (www.learngreatfoods.com).

Don't let your broker "sweep" your cash away.

Most stockbrokers have accounts that allow you to keep and use a certain amount of cash along with the stocks, bonds and funds you buy and hold in the account. The cash balance grows or declines based on how much you invest and how much you put into the account. No surprises there. The surprise happens when it comes to the interest rate paid on that cash. It can be practically nothing—unless you tell your broker otherwise. Reason: they set up the so-called "sweep" account—the cash account facilitating stock buys and sells—usually in the lowest interest product they offer. You can have them move it to a money market fund or even a government-securities-based money fund for safety, which pays more—but most make you ask for that. So ask for it— don't leave good money on the broker's table.

"Take care of the pence, and the pounds will take care of themselves."

—Lord Chesterfield

Learn what others say about saving money.

You'll find (or may have already found) that there are a whole lot of people like us writing about ways to save money—in books, magazines, newspapers, on the Internet, and so on. Look closely, and you'll find a lot of good ideas, all collected from the millions of us who experience life on a daily basis. Don't ignore these new ideas (yeah, some of them are old, too; you'll learn to recognize the new ones pretty quickly). Read magazines like *Real Simple* and *Consumer Reports* every now and then—in the library, at the doctor's office (we stop short of recommending a subscription). Bookmark a few moneysaving Web sites and check them out occasionally. Consumer Tips and Reports (www.consumertipsreports. org) and Get Rich Slowly (www.getrichslowly.org) are good not-for-profits with plenty of advice and real world experience to share.

Don't buy features you don't need.

Want a new cell phone? A new car? A new TV? Heck, even a new DVD player? The temptation, always, at least with most of us, is to get all the bells and whistles. Touch-screen keypads, navigation systems, thirteen different ways to input digital media, surround sound—you know the drill. And most of us will find, if we do empty our wallets and fatten the retail coffers by springing for these things, we'll never use them anyway, even if our ten-year-olds show us how! Best bet: Stick to what you really need. If you think you'll use a feature less than 10 or 20 percent of the time, just don't buy it.

Use that corporate discount—for personal travel.

If you travel a lot on business, you've probably noticed that a lot of hotels charge the "corporate rate" when you travel for your company. Pretty good discounts, too, especially for foreign hotels. But did you know that you can—usually—make use of these discounts for your own personal travel? Sure. The hotels don't ask questions; for the most part, they're just happy to have your business. Simply ask for the corporate rate when you book, and be prepared to show them your company ID when you check in, if they happen to ask.

Write effective complaint letters.

Sometimes you're just not able to resolve a dispute effectively—in person or especially with a phone agent. Often you're dealing with people who are paid by the number of people they serve, not how well they serve them, and they aren't empowered to do anything anyway. So sometimes it comes down to writing a letter. In a letter, 1) you demonstrate you're sincere, 2) you can lay the facts and history out logically and concisely and 3) you and the company you're dealing with end up with a permanent record of the discussion. Like most other communication, there's a right way and a wrong way to go about it. There isn't enough space to go into detail here, but do a search on "how to write an effective complaint letter" and you'll get lots of help—a good example is at www.writeexpress.com/complaint.htm.

Buy these three items in bulk.

Keep an eye out for sales on these long-lasting staples that can be used to make a variety of dishes: 1) canned beans—garbanzo, pinto, kidney, or black—which you can use in all kinds of salads and casseroles; 2) rice, which lasts forever; and 3) chicken stock—buy cans whenever they are marked down (often around the holidays) and use them to make your own quick soups throughout the year.

Dine at off-peak times.

Check out www.dinnerbroker.com to see if there are restaurants in your area that will offer discounted meals if booked at off-peak times.

Recycle eyeglass frames.

No need to buy a new pair of frames every time your prescription changes. Your optician can use the same frames and replace the glass with the new prescription lenses, saving you hundreds of dollars.

Don't be dazzled by designer jeans.

Designer jeans in a clothing store can cost upwards of $150—way upwards. But if you have a yearning for the fancy jean brands, head straight to the thrift store and designer consignment stores. You will find many top brands hanging on the racks for far less than you'd pay in a fancy store.

Try discounted meat.

Look carefully in the meat counter to see if there is any meat drastically reduced for quick sale. Don't worry; it is perfectly healthy. In-store butchers have to mark the meat down to move it as it approaches its "sell by" date, and you can get tremendous bargains. If you can't find a reduced-price section in your store, ask at the meat counter.

Take a tip from the tip jar.

Even Google is getting into the money-saving game. They've started a "tip jar" where users can send their best money-saving ideas. Like on *American Idol,* the best ideas will float to the top. Check out www.google.com/tipjar/ to see what folks are sending in today.

Got one going to college? Prepare for the SAT cheap—or free!

Taking the SAT has become the standard rite of passage for college admission for most students. And it can be expensive. Time was, you paid for the test, showed up on the Saturday morning, took the test, waited for the results, and hoped for the best. Nowadays, college entrance has become so competitive that many families spend literally thousands on test prep and tutoring services. While some of that may make sense, and there are also some good books out there, you should also be aware that the College Board (the folks who design and administer the tests) have a lot of free test prep resources—including practice tests—on their Web site (www.collegeboard.com). And while scoring well is important, remember that this is an aptitude test, so there's a limit to how much a total immersion study program will really help.

Save first. Spend later.

Park your credit cards. If there is something you want to buy, save up the cash before you buy it. Whether you start a special savings account that you designate for your saved funds, or just put a bunch of bills in an envelope with the purpose written on the outside, the point is to wait until you can afford to buy with cash. You just might find that by the time you have the money saved up, you've lost interest, or the price might have dropped!

Reconsider pet supplements.

The ads are compelling, but your pets really don't need to take vitamins and other diet supplements. If they are otherwise healthy and you are feeding them well, skip the costly supplements.

Go local. Transfer global.

In the good old days, if you went to college you packed your bags and headed to some nice bucolic college town to live the college life, from freshman year forward—four years or more, full tuition and living expenses, the college life. And you were expected to do that if you wanted to be considered a college graduate in full standing. But nowadays with escalating college costs, crowded universities and increasing availability and funding (in many states, anyway) of community colleges, it can make a lot of sense to pick up basic requirements at a local institution. Most community colleges offer clear transition paths to the larger universities in that state, and most now offer much of the rich experience, the culture and college life, of their larger brethren. Parents and prospective students should check out this route; you can still become a doctor or a Nobel laureate via the local alternative.

Make the most of advanced placement.

You have a college-bound kid in high school? Make sure you check out the "advanced placement" courses and programs. Advanced placement ("AP") has been around for years, and it can be a real money-saver to get AP credit for a college course you'd otherwise have to pay for. Also, placing out of a basic course allows the student to take more electives and may even avoid scheduling and sequencing bottlenecks that can make the supposed four-year degree take much longer. So if college is on the horizon, take full advantage of AP opportunities.

Want a scholarship? Leave no stone unturned.

If you're depending on financial aid to send your kids to college, you're in good company—some two-thirds of the population, in fact, are in the same boat. And if you're getting close to the fateful day of writing that first tuition check, you've probably worked the financial-aid landscape pretty hard, likely with the aid of counseling staff at your school of choice. Those counselors are well versed in the traditional aid sources, from government grant and aid programs to scholarships through the school's alumni association. But they may or may not tap into the organizations that you are part of. Check out scholarship programs offered by your company or any professional organization you may be a part of—you just might be the perfect candidate they're looking for.

Don't replace—repair your shoes.

Shoes are made to last, and they can last even longer if you keep them polished and cleaned. New heels and tips can easily keep a pair of shoes going for another year, putting off the moment when you really will wear them out and have to buy new ones. Boots can be made to last a lifetime, and every few years the shoe repair person can spiff them up to keep them going in style.

Keep your freezer full and your fridge empty.

Okay, this sounds kind of weird—if the idea is to keep your food cold, why would your freezer work differently than your refrigerator? Because the fridge depends on circulation to cool food, while the freezer works better when it can turn everything into one giant block of ice. Don't ask too many questions—that's just the way it is.

Try out Grandma's oatmeal hamburgers.

No, we really don't expect you to make hamburgers out of oatmeal, but you do need to know that your grandmother made her ground beef go further by adding oatmeal to it. When making a meatloaf, you can add bulk by using three-fourths of a cup of oatmeal for every pound of hamburger meat.

To replace—or not to replace—an appliance?

Most of us have a pretty good idea how long a car should last, although it's been getting longer in recent years (did you know the median car age has risen to 9.4 years—according to R.J. Polk?—there's a money-saving message there, too). Anyway, most of us are probably less cognizant of how long an appliance, say your fridge, your dishwasher, your washer and dryer, your microwave—should last. So just as there's a Web site for everything, yes, there's a Web site for this, too. Check out http://www.demesne.info/Home-Maintenance/Appliance-Life-Expectancy.htm. Also, another indicator that it could be time to replace the appliance (other than the obvious clue of a large repair bill) is its energy efficiency. If it's not an "EnergyStar" appliance, it might be time. See if you can find that old EnergyStar label with the owner's manual, and take the time to compare energy use with the current models.

"Make do and mend."

—Wartime slogan from the 1940s

If you can save sales tax, do it.

Sales tax, in most states anyway, adds anywhere from 5 percent to as much as 9 percent to the price of our purchases. Most of us spend hundreds a year on it; even more if we buy a car or make some other major purchase. So it's worth saving a few bucks here and there when you can. How? One way is buying online or from out-of-state mail-order sources. Now, it doesn't always work, and you have to check the situation—the law says if a company has any operation in your state, even a shipping warehouse, they must collect tax on your purchase. Some companies collect these taxes voluntarily. And many states make you liable for "use" taxes if you buy out of state, but there's no enforcement mechanism, and most such taxes go unpaid. Many states allow you to carry out a meal tax-free—it is considered buying food, like groceries, which are generally not taxable. You should at least research the tax-free alternative, keeping in mind the situations where tax is paid anyway, and keeping shipping costs in mind.

Use pet food coupons.

To get a discount on pet food and other pet-related products from giant producer Purina, check out www.purina.com. When we visited the site you could get a free can of Mighty Dog dog food.

Store your files online for free.

Small businesses can store and share documents for free with Microsoft's Office Live. Check it out at www.smallbusiness .officelive.com.

Cruise for bargain prices.

If you can wait until just a few weeks before departure, you can get much better prices on cruises, sometimes up to 75 percent off the regular brochure price. Check out www .vacationstogo.com, and look in the sections marked 90 Day Ticker and Find a Bargain.

Invest in something that pays you back.

Sometimes it is worth it to buy an item, an expensive item that will slowly earn back its cost and more. Examples are an espresso machine, if it keeps you out of the coffee line, or a clothes steamer, if it keeps you from sending your shirts to the cleaners to be pressed. This only works if you use the item regularly, of course. Many an expensive treadmill (purchased to cut back on the money you spend at the gym) ends up as an extra place to hang your pants rather than an actual piece of exercise equipment.

Print both sides.

Keep a supply of used printer paper—the letters you never sent, the flyers that were wrong, the letterhead where your name is spelled wrong—and use it a second time in your printer for any rough drafts you are printing.

Buy global, pick up local.

Need a new flat screen TV? Of course, buying one in the first place isn't a way to save money. But there are ways to save once you make up your mind that you need it and can afford it. Now, it's on to the most cost-effective way to buy it. Certainly you watch the ads, review the reviews, and try to find the best price. And these days there's a good chance the best deal will be found online. But especially for something as big as a TV, the price of the TV is hardly the end of the story. You have tax, and then there's the shipping too. Here's where it makes most sense—and more big chain stores are offering this option—to pick out what you want, buy it online, and reserve it for pickup at the nearest store. First, this is easy, especially if you already know what you want. Second, you don't get a pushy salesman trying to sell you an extended warranty or some other add-on. Third, you save shipping charges. And fourth, if something goes wrong, you have a place to take it back to, no charge, no hassle. Peter did this recently and very successfully with Sears—it works.

Spend time instead of money.

If you gave money to charity before and now feel too strapped to be generous with your cash, why not be generous with your time. Show up and help out, and you will still feel like you are contributing. If you are between professional jobs, it can be a great way to keep your skills up and feel useful.

Stay put.

Stay put in your marriage—it's a great way to save money. The only people who profit from divorce are lawyers. Everyone else takes huge financial hits, something that you should work hard to avoid nowadays. If your budget is strained now, it will be strained even further if you try to maintain two separate households.

Look upon the next few years as an opportunity to work together to get through this challenging period. Remember that the authors of the book *The Millionaire Next Door* found in their research that most wealthy people have one thing in common—they married once, and stayed put.

Make it a game.

Don't think of saving money and spending less as a chore when it can be a game. The whole family can participate in trying to be the best of the super-savers. Take this new way of life on as a challenge, as a way to learn new skills, and to get the most for your money now and in the future.

Don't do this yourself.

We've given you lots of ideas on how and where to save money. There are, however, things that you just don't want to do yourself, as it will cost far more to fix it if you botch the job. Like . . . your eyebrows, don't wax them yourself. So before you set out to fix your car, redo your floors, dig up your pipes, ask yourself—is there a chance this will cost me more in the long run? If you aren't certain of your abilities, if it is a high-stakes task, the budget-minded choice might be to hire a professional to do it for you.

"Money is not required to buy one necessity of the soul."

—Henry David Thoreau

It isn't your job to fix the economy—don't feel like you have to spend to help out.

Most of us are good, patriotic Americans, able and willing to do most anything to help our country. That's a good thing. But there's a tendency, in bad economic times, to feel an urge to "do your duty" to help out. We feel the urge to break the so-called "savings paradox," where during tough times people simply stop spending—which causes more hard times. We feel the urge to buy American. We feel the urge to support a business run by our next-door neighbor. We're lured to spend by so many bargains and sales by so many businesses trying to keep going. We hear that XYZ restaurant down the street might be in trouble. We hear that people are getting laid off at the corner grocery. We see for-sale and for-lease signs everywhere. We get special stimulus "rebate" checks accompanied by a message to spend to help the economy. Heck, it's hard enough to control spending anyway—how do we feel when all these factors start to creep out of the woodwork to haunt us? Never be "guilted" into spending money.

The best practice, in bad times and good, is to be aware, be committed, and be in control of our spending habits. To spend less than we earn, to save for a rainy day, to buy smart when we buy. Nobody can survive without buying anything; the trick is to know what to buy, when to buy it, and how much to pay. Life is so much better when you can control spending enough to make ends meet during the bad times. Then you have extra to save or spend on something really special during the good times. Yet, most of us tune our finances to just break even during the good times—which naturally gets us into trouble when the bad times return. If you tune your finances to make ends meet in bad times, you're well on the way to building sustained financial success. The 573 tips you just read about should help you do that.

Index

hair styling, 178
laser treatment bargains,
210
tinted moisturizer, 167
use sunscreen, 169
using kitchen ingredients,
211
Beecher, Henry Ward, 144
beekeeping, 193
Ben and Jerry's ice cream, 139
Berra, Yogi, 196
beverages. *See also* coffee; wine;
bottled water, 40
soda, 191
Bibles, free, 132
bicycles, 105
buying, 129
Bierce, Ambrose, 93
bills, paying. *See also* credit
cards, 33
autopaying, 236
"prompt pay" discounts, 170
books
book-swap club, 48
reading aloud, 69
bowling, 216
bread, 124, 185
bread pudding, 161
making, 5, 141
Brecher, John, 205
Brees, Karen, 178
brunch, 139, 248
Burpee's "Money Garden"
packet, 233
business cards, 181

businesses, small or home-
based, 164
freelance writing, 233
free marketing ideas, 180
free online files storage/
sharing, 269
paper-saving ideas, 179
using your children, 184
Butters, Mary Jane, 212

C

Caesar salad, 246
calculators, using, 190
Campbell Soup company, 21
candles, hand-rolled, 28
CarMax, 54, 87
carpets, cleaning, 39
homemade freshener, 41
cars
buying used, 87
carpooling, 49
changing air filter, 2
checking gas cap, 226
cleaning out trunk, 83
combining errands, 181, 226
having only one, 102
inflating tires, 1
insurance, 34, 56, 89, 95
keeping longer, 34
"no-drive" days, 31
park in shade, 227
Rent-a-Wreck, 183
ride-share cars, 206
speed and mpg, 48, 122
use regular gas, 1

S

salads, 51, 246
   salad dressings, 141
   using wild greens, 13
salt, 165
Schardt, Katie, 245
scholarships, college, 265
Schor, Juliet B., 57
scratch paper, 106
Seneca, 207
sewing, 180
Shakespeare & Company, 208
Shaw, Henry Wheeler, 216
Sherman, Spencer, 102
shipping costs, saving, 218,
   219, 229
shoes, 149
   repairing, 266
   taking off inside, 253
   using shoe boxes, 108
shopping. *See also* grocery
   stores, 54, 58, 146
   antique and flea markets, 22
   asking for discounts/specials,
     12, 107, 170
   avoid extra features, 259
   buying used items, 19
   buying used rental
     equipment, 125
   consignment stores, 22
   dollar stores, 197
   and driving route, 103
   factory outlets, 86
   garage sales, 16
   holiday sales, 16
   no impulse buying, 234
   online, 94, 170, 204,
     247, 270
   outlet malls, 216
   out of season for big
     items, 15
   pay with cash, 263
   prioritizing "wants" or
     "needs," 95, 98, 102
   renting seasonal or one-
     time use items, 8
   rummage sales, 175
   saving sales tax, 268
   using coupons, 36
   wait before buying, 43,
     98, 104
showers, 35
   low-flow showerhead, 40
Shuppert, Karen, 51
Skype, 61
Slobe, Bob, 1
slow cookers, 137
   solar, 4
Smith, Will, 114
Smithsonian Magazine, 23
smoking, 148
soda, 191
soup, making, 47
spas or salons. *See also*
   personal care; beauty tips
   home spas, 26
   price break and number of
     services, 18
SPIN farming, 51
sports clubs, 182

rental cars in Europe, 248
road trips, 86
sharing rentals, 164
sleep free in Paris, 208
"staycation," 83
staying in dorm rooms, 38
staying in hostels, 117
staying in private
    home, 105
using local grocery
    stores, 74
using public transportation,
    75
volunteer, 49
where dollar is strong, 182
vacuum cleaner bags, 244
Venice, visiting, 246
video games, 81
volunteering, 271
    for "reference accounts,"
        257
    word-of-mouth marketing,
        117

W
walking, 44, 68, 196
Walmart, free samples from,
    133
warranty, extended, 53
water, bottled, 40

water heaters, 139
weatherstripping, 72
websites. See Internet; specific
    topics
weddings
    budget dresses, 209
    cost of, 184, 185, 243
    gifts for, 254
weed killer, 251
weight, losing, 99, 223
Weil, Simone, 229
Wesley, John, 85
Wilde, Stuart, 58
Wilson, Earl, 12, 14, 110, 186
wine
    bringing to restaurants, 92
    by the case, 267
    "Chardonnay" tax, 205
    glass size, 142
    half-bottles, 9
    Prosecco, 47
    wine-tasting parties, 28
women, do-it-yourself info for,
    214, 234
worms, using, 213
writing, freelance, 233

Z
Zipcars, 206

About the Authors

Peter and Jennifer Sander are the authors or co-authors of more than twenty books, including *The Pocket Idiot's Guide to Living on a Budget* and *Green Christmas*. Peter is the author of *Madoff* (The Globe Pequot Press, 2009) and *The 250 Personal Finance Questions Everyone Should Ask*. He has an MBA, has developed more than 200 personal finance columns for MarketWatch and TheStreet .com, and has appeared on NBC's *Today*, CNNfn, and Fox News. Jennifer Basye Sander is America's Affordable Luxury Expert. Through her books and speeches, she reveals the many ways that a family can live well on less. A *New York Times*-bestselling author, she teaches non-fiction writing in Northern California. They live with their two sons in Granite Bay, California.